Teaching

during the

Jurassic

Wit and Wisdom from an
Old Hippie Teacher

Teaching

during the

Jurassic

Wit and Wisdom from an
Old Hippie Teacher

Martin Settle

atmosphere press

Table of Contents

Acknowledgements

Just as with a child, it takes a village to raise a book. I have many people to thank for their encouragement and suggestions – too many to name, in fact. But I will name those that made the greatest contributions: Taylor Bowler, as a reader, editor, and coffee buddy; Vicki Derderian, as a reader and editor; John Adams as a reader and former student, now a best friend; Jackie Fishman, as reader and fellow lover of Malbec; and Larry and Kirby Settle, as readers and the best brothers a guy could have.

Always, always I must acknowledge the atmosphere of support and love that my spouse Deborah Bosley supplies. Without these, the world is flat.

To all K-12 teachers, who have carried on with excellence despite poor pay, little appreciation, and roadblocks from administrators and politicians. Your contributions are great and your legacies long.

Preface

Teaching during the Jurassic is part memoir, part philosophical commentary, and part guide to those entering the teaching profession. The *Jurassic* of the title refers to the period that I taught high school English from the late 1960s up to the early 1990s. Of course, the use of *Jurassic* is hyperbolic, but this period seems subjectively eons ago and the changes that have occurred during this time geologic. There were no personal computers, cell phones, the internet, gay marriage, an African American President of two terms, school shootings by the score, "No child left behind," etc. during my time at the helm of a classroom.

As a memoir, the people and places within are real; their names are not. Those who are still alive to verify these stories can easily enough figure out some of the real identities of the characters and places that run across these pages. Further, the memoir part of *Teaching during Jurassic* is thematically based and not chronologically arranged. Each chapter takes on a particular theme, which will draw from many places and incidents along a timeline.

While I do have historical times and dates in this book, most of the stories are less about historical accuracy than revealing the values and attitudes of the times. Some anecdotes are humorous, with caveats to the reader that I might have been fired if I were teaching today. There was a looser atmosphere in the schools of my time and a looser supervision. A high school teacher was like a subcontractor and was autonomous in much of what he or she did. We could get away with a lot for good or ill.

Some of the stories are tragic, which should not be surprising since I was dealing with the lives of adolescents, who have a knack for doing impulsive things that lead to dire consequences. Then, there are those stories that have implications for educational philosophy and pedagogy, including strategies on how to be a subversive teacher and still thrive in a public educational system.

Teaching during the Jurassic, while having its moments of nostalgia, does not praise everything that occurred during those years. There's much that is realistic here and much about these times that deserves criticism. Even in my disappointment of the present era of education in the public schools, I do not point to "the-good-old-days" as a model for the future. Quite the contrary, I believe that we have not gotten far enough away from the past. We're presently stuck in an age of *efficiency* and *accountability* – last refuges of the unimaginative.

Every age has its salient work. The period between 1960 and 1990 was an age of multiculturalism. New ways of looking at gender, race, ethnicity, and sexuality reached a fever pitch. All of the issues surrounding these movements filtered down into the classroom. Grammar was altered to accommodate feminism and Ebonics, the literary canon suddenly included a host of new books by authors from a wide variety of cultural backgrounds, and textbooks were revised to make room for contributions from diverse segments of our population. During my tenure, it was exciting and provocative to be a part of the changes that were occurring in education. That is not to say that that the issues of my time in the classroom aren't still a work progress today, but they were incipient during the Jurassic.

While there are materials in education that are times-specific, there are many universals in *Teaching during the Jurassic*. The chapter called "The Outsiders" is about a phenomenon that all secondary teachers encounter and worry about. What to do about the students that don't fit in? It is achingly painful to see most of these kids trying to make their way through such a closed, peer-group-driven system. I tried to let the "outsiders" know (most of the time with little success) that the high school bus terminal is a brief stopover on the trip to adulthood, and that they soon would be heading to more welcoming climes.

For the most part, these "outsider students" are not dangerous to others, although they may be dangerous to themselves. However, there is always a small percentage of them that are *really* dangerous students. I had pre-Columbine students that would have been capable of shooting up the school. Thank god, they had no precedent to do so, because I did know they had guns. In this chapter, I go into more detail about one such dangerous student.

It would be my fondest hope that the readers of this book, especially the newcomers to teaching, come to realize they are engaging with a lifelong learner. My devotion to learning has been unending from high school to retirement. There is nothing I like more than the frissons of academic discovery. *Teaching during the Jurassic* is full of references to the great thinkers of that time period – Marshall McLuhan, R. Buckminster Fuller, Neil Postman, Saul Alinsky, Joseph Campbell, Stephen Jay Gould, B. F. Skinner, and more. Moreover, as a teacher of literature, I think the reader will find this work chock full of quotes and allusions of a literary nature. And there's poetry in this work to break any of the listlessness that might come from the carbohydrates of prose – some of the poetry is from well-known poets and some mine.

Please, don't conclude that I'm all about academics in a formal sort of way. There are many places in *Teaching during the Jurassic* where I get a bit bawdy. That comes from my past as a bartender in my family's restaurant, where liquor and the profane mixed well together. The chapter "What Your Education Courses Never Taught You" gets a little down and dirty using Saul Alinsky's idea for a fart-in and Benjamin Franklin's scientific paper called "Fart Proudly." I am a devotee of humor, and I have written a joke book. There is no chapter in this book that does not come down from lofty heights to the echoing valleys of laughter. As Mark Twain would say, "Humor is mankind's greatest blessing."

According to Virginia Woolf, "On or about December 1910, human character changed" – a rather arbitrary date for the beginning of Modernism. Historical turning points are seldom tidy, but it works well enough. If I had to pick a date like Virginia Woolf did, I would choose August 6, 1991. This is the day that the World Wide Web without any fanfare was publicly introduced to the world. The character of students and education would begin to significantly change after that date. I point to this date and see it rather subjectively as marking the end of my Jurassic period. After this, I would become a dinosaur, who couldn't distinguish a pixel from a pixie.

I would not like to contend, which is the thesis of *Teaching during the Jurassic*, that I am an unhappy creature nor an irrelevant creature from another age. Since August 6, 1991, the Jurassic has been made more visible to me, with its complex mixture of social goals, technology, pedagogy, and cultural attitudes. "Things reveal themselves passing away," according to William Butler Yeats. I can see clearly now the outlines of what used to be and, while I believe that much from the Jurassic should be disposed of, much is still applicable to the present and to the future. *Teaching during the Jurassic* is both a preservation of what came before and a plea for more comprehensive changes for education in the future.

Get out your pencils – or whatever you use – and do what *real* readers do: mark up and argue with *Teaching during the Jurassic*.

Chapter 1
The End of the Beginning

"The Bolt"

Miss Hermione Boltz had been an English teacher for forty years. "The Bolt" – that's what I called her – was a stout woman with a face like a bulldog. She had never married and her dedication to teaching was of a stern, gray cloth like the Puritans of the Salem community.

From the very beginning, we didn't hit it off. This was to be the last semester of her long and solemn career, and I was to be her last chance to pass on her sorcery to a student teacher. My coordinating teacher from the college, Dr. Crawford, introduced us on an icy winter day, and I can't say that the atmosphere thawed when we met in her office.

I could see she was appalled by my appearance – a head of hair that made me look like a mad scientist because it wouldn't hold an Afro; bell-bottom jeans; a tie-dye shirt; a leather belt with a large buckle; and a leather bracelet with the peace sign stamped on it. The era of the hippie had arrived, and The Bolt was about as much in sympathy with it as she was with a rabid dog. If she had hair on her back (which she may have had), it would have stood straight up.

After our initial stilted hellos, the first question that she had was what I had been reading lately – a fair enough question from one English major to another. I was reading the latest issue of *Evergreen Review* (an avant-garde literary magazine) and a lesser-known novel by Jack Kerouac titled *The Subterraneans*. In kind, to create a little rapport, I asked about her reading. She was reading the essays of Addison and Steele in *The Spectator* and re-reading Boswell's biography of Samuel Johnson. Ooo-kay – a two-hundred-and-fifty-year gap between our literary interests. I was Kerouac and Cassady and she was Johnson and Boswell.

Since it didn't look like we were going to banter about our reading, "The Bolt" got down to brass tacks. She gave me copies of her syllabi and reading lists. She would be teaching three sections of a British lit survey course to college-bound seniors, and two sections of a world lit class to non-college-bound sophomores. Glancing over both syllabi, I felt that I was already familiar with most of the works that were being referenced. At least, that was a relief.

She told me my first two weeks in her class were strictly going to be observational so that I could learn the methods of the master. When she found that I had learned enough about how she ran her classes, she would gradually give me more responsibilities. Ultimately, if I had progressed sufficiently after that, she told me that I could teach extended sections of the syllabi to her classes.

By way of her personal dress code, I was to get a haircut and come to class in a shirt and tie with dress pants. I was about to protest these demands when Dr. Crawford spiked one of my feet with her high heels. "Of course, Miss Boltz, Marty will be glad to accommodate in any way that you think appropriate."

I grimaced and grunted my agreement to Dr. Crawford's statement, "Your wish is my command, Miss Blotz."

She stared at me. "It's Boltz, not Blotz."

"Ah, yes. Like 'nuts and bolts.' I should be able to remember that."

She continued to stare.

We concluded our meeting with the details of arrival times and parking. I could tell student teaching was going to be a dodgy experience, but I did take comfort that "The Bolt" was clear and concise in her expectations, and I should be able to deal with that. Dr. Crawford and I left in silence and crunched to the parking lot through the snow. When we got into her car, all she said was, "Marty, suck it up."

Observations and Perturbations

I arrived an hour early on my first day of student teaching. The locker doors slamming, the roar of hundreds of conversations, the various social groupings from jocks to thugs to cheerleaders, and the high-pitched screams from the girls (something that I never got used to throughout my teaching career) were a flashback to my high school days, which were really only four years previous. I made my way in nostalgia and fascination to Miss Boltz's classroom.

She was already there organizing her handouts and putting homework on the board. Among the notes on the board by way of introduction was my name. She looked up with a sigh at my sartorial splendor. I had gotten a haircut and wore a dress shirt with tie and dress pants. These were my concessions. But I wore a hand-painted Hawaiian tie with a hula dancer on it, no belt, and tennis shoes. There was a noticeable pause before she decided that there wasn't time for another lecture on professional appearance.

One thing I must say about Miss Boltz, she was thoroughly prepared with detailed lesson plans, classroom policies from which there were no deviations, and a studied familiarity with the material that she was presenting. On the first day of class, she introduced me to all of her sections. I was her helper and passed out syllabi and reading lists. Like the students, I had an assigned seat in the back corner of the room, where I could observe the techniques of my mentor.

The first two weeks of class – my strictly observational period – went by quickly, despite a certain amount of boredom watching Miss Boltz do three classes on the same topic followed by two other classes on the same topic. I dutifully observed her classes, took copious notes and, most importantly, kept my mouth shut. Before, between, and after classes, she taught and supervised me while I learned the organizational skills of lesson plans, taking roll, making tests, grading tests, and entering grades – all very practical skills and all very useful.

However, during my two-week initiation, I did observe a few stylistic and philosophical differences in handling material and students. While Miss Boltz did know her material well, she always presented it in a sanitized way. Wordsworth in her hands had a sweetness that I wouldn't have chosen to emphasize – or at least I would have made some comparisons between his nature poetry and his protest poetry. But Hermione Boltz was only interested in Wordsworth's mystical response to nature.

This led to, perhaps, one of the most embarrassing moments of my teaching career. In an act of apparent spontaneity (I'm sure she had planned it, though) she chose the new student teacher (yours truly) to give a rendering of Wordsworth's poem "I Wandered Lonely as a Cloud." The poem was about the poet coming across a bunch of daffodils on a nature walk and getting all dewy-eyed about it. To add to the verisimilitude of the moment, "The Bolt" had brought a plastic daffodil to class, which she entreated me to hold – I suppose she thought that this prop would help me try to recreate Wordsworth's ecstasy at finding these flowers and later recalling them in tranquility. I could tell the students were quite aware of the awkwardness of this situation for me. None of them laughed aloud, but I could see mighty struggles going to keep their composures. My face had turned a red verging on purple and my voice struggled to give the lofty tones necessary for the occasion. As far as I was concerned, I may as well have been dressed in motley. As far as "The Bolt" was concerned, I *was* dressed in motley.

Another observation of our contrasting personalities, Hermione appealed to and had a following of young high school women that enjoyed regressing to a sexless world of pretend. It was like they were trying to recreate their childhood of playing house and dress-up. Boltz had a tea club for them (no nasty boys allowed) that met once a week during lunch hour. They tried to re-enact the salon atmosphere of the English teas of Johnson and Boswell, sometimes wearing period hats and dresses. After class, these girls flocked around her like a host of...well, daffodils.

In a contrary way, I have always appealed to young men, and my approach to literature was less refined and more rugged. Instead of "emotions recollected in tranquility," I was more into the bold emotions of the revolutionary. I would have read Wordsworth's "The Discharged Soldier" alongside the daffodil poem, since we were in the midst of the Vietnam war and "flower power." My approach was steeped in the tumultuous present; Miss Boltz was more into the golden dimensions of past centuries. Also, I was more iconoclastic, immersed in the 60's defiance of authority. I would have told students that unfortunately William Wordsworth lived too long and produced volumes of the worst poetry known to humankind. "The Idiot Boy" gets my vote for one of the worst sentiments ever found in poetry.

The most disturbing of my observations of Miss Boltz's cluster of characteristics was her response to the age of the "hippie." As I have reported previously, she did not care for my long hair or my attire. Not unusual for a person from her generation. However, she let her disgust spill over into the classroom. After two weeks of observing her class, I noticed she NEVER called on male students with long hair either for an answer or for a request for information. They were like non-persons in communist Russia. She would often look out over the class for hands raised. Even if one of the hippie students had the only hand raised, she would not acknowledge it. The first two or three times I saw this behavior, I wanted to point out to her there was a hand raised. Soon, like me, these "hippie" students realized it was futile to ask or answer questions. They, also, realized it was futile to get an "A."

While I was observing, "The Bolt" assigned me *my* homework assignment, which was to prepare a week's worth of lesson plans for her World Lit sophomores. Since they had arrived at The Renaissance and The Enlightenment section of their texts, I would be in charge of introducing them to the state of Illinois' required *Julius Caesar* by William Shakespeare. I wasn't particularly happy about the topic – I was (and continued to be) a reluctant promoter of the Bard for high school students. However, it was a better gig than teaching the *Epic of Gilgamesh*, which would have been assigned if I had taught the first semester.

Tragedy and Freytag's Pyramid

The moment had arrived. I was to be unleashed to teach my first classes – two sections of sophomore World Literature. The topic: Shakespeare's *Julius Caesar*. I checked my notes and zipper, took roll, and left the safety of the shore. "The Bolt" sat in the back of the class, waiting to right the ship if it became necessary.

As you might expect, I was not myself. Too much was at stake for me to be loose or experimental. I had to prove to Miss Boltz – not the students – that I was a competent educator. My show was meticulously choreographed without any moments of improvisation:

- background on Shakespeare and Elizabethan England (check)

- the historic Julius Caesar (check)
- handout and demonstration of Freytag's Pyramid (check)
- assign Act I of the play (unannounced pop quiz tomorrow) (check)
- do not make eye contact with Miss Boltz (check)

The only awkward moment in my opening act was that I actually called on a student with long hair. There was a pregnant moment when all heads in class turned to look at "The Bolt," but she was looking down taking notes. One could sense a frisson of relief circulating around the room. After the day was done, Hermione seemed pleased with my performance. And I believed that I was beginning to win her over.

All went well during the week. I kept to my robotic style of teaching, gave quizzes, and graded papers. I enforced all her policies on the syllabus and accepted no deviations. In fact, things were going so well that "The Bolt" decided to leave me on my own on the last day of the week so that she could attend to some work she needed to do.

I had resolved not to let this freedom go to my head. Part of the class was going to be recitations of Mark Antony's famous funeral oration – "Friends, Romans, Countrymen, lend me your ears." I sensed that this exercise demanded by Miss Boltz was not going to be easy for this age group. Sophomores in high school had delicate egos, even though they carried themselves with a cool "self-confidence." To stand-up in the scrutiny of their peers and stumble through Mark Antony's speech would be comparable to coming to class with toilet paper trailing one's shoes. My classes in the future would give students the option of writing down or reciting memorized material, but this was not an option for Miss Boltz.

This exercise was fraught with dangers, and I knew many would choose to lose the points for the exercise rather than suffer the slings and arrows of outrageous fortune. The stress was palpable. Unfortunately, my answer to stress has always been levity. I gave them an improvisational version of the speech to break the ice with "lend me some beer" and "I have come to praise her berries and not to seize them." In addition, I performed this oration using a lisp. Before I knew it, I had opened up a sluice in both myself and the students. Laughter fell not like the gentle dew from heaven but like a torrential rain. After that, I just let go, cracking jokes left and right, but still accomplishing the goal of recitation. If one were to plot this class as if it were a part of a Tragedy on Freytag's Pyramid, it would have been the climax followed by falling action.

When I arrived at Miss Boltz's office at the end of the day, I could tell things were amiss. Quoting from Shakespeare in *Cariolanus*, I saw that "The tartness of his [her] face sours ripe grapes." Her first words were, "Mrs. Arnold reported to me that she heard raucous laughter coming out of your classroom." I had to admit this was true.

"Brenda Attwood (one of Bolt's snitch, flower girls) said that you referred to William Shakespeare as Bill, and that you did a rendition of Mark Antony's speech with a lisp."

"Yeth." (I had become irrepressible).

"I think you need to return to your observational mode for a while. I don't think you have the seriousness that is required for the profession you seek to enter."

"But I accomplished the goals of class, Hermione."

"*Never* call me 'Hermione.'"

As a result of that so fair and foul a day, I never again taught a class without Miss Boltz's presence. Nor was I ever given an opportunity to despoil the minds of her college-bound seniors about to launch into high academe. I had broken a bond of a sacred trust and would be on permanent probation – *mea culpa, mea culpa, mea maxima culpa.*

Because I was relegated to the back of the class and because my opportunities to teach were greatly diminished, I got to listen to Miss Boltz on a daily basis. It's not that her lectures were totally boring (and she did lecture as was the approach of the times), but that I got to hear her British Literature lectures three times in a row. By the third class, I felt that I could teach the material myself with some useful additions. She never let me go to the library alone to work. I guess she felt that she had to keep an eye on me. I tried to keep myself occupied by grading papers and entering grades, but there were many times that I had nothing to do but listen and squirm.

I think that the incident of the "Friday Laughter Massacre" had put an end to any hopes she had that I was trainable. I shared some of my concerns with my coordinating teacher Dr. Crawford. She did all she could to encourage Miss Boltz to give me more chances. She extolled the work that I did as a student at the university. But it was all to no avail. "The Bolt" not only looked like a bulldog, but she clamped down hard on me like a bulldog.

She was unfazed by pleas for second chances or suggestions that I might be used in unique ways to communicate with the present generation. At most, I thought, if I kept my nose clean and my mouth sealed, I would be able to get out of the situation with a "B."

Coup de Grace

My demise began with laughter and ended with laughter – a tinkly, subdued laughter. I couldn't tell if it came from a dream or if it was real. All I knew was that I was warm and comfortable until I heard a familiar voice, "Isn't that true, Mr. Settle?"

"Wa...wa?"

The laughter became more palpable, and I realized it was external. I opened one eye and then, I realized that I was in Miss Boltz's third British Literature class, and the voice was Miss Boltz's. I snapped to attention so quickly that my books spewed off the desk and onto the floor. The laughter became near hysterical at that point.

The classroom had been especially warm that day, and the lecture had been particularly boring. I had fought sleep for half the period with the snapping-head response like a driver that should pull over and take a rest, but I eventually succumbed to the arms of Morpheus. I was out like a lotus-eater. By the time I gathered my books and reached consciousness, Miss Boltz had moved on, leaving me with the knowledge that I had done the unforgivable – I had fallen asleep on my watch. The only comment that Miss Boltz made after class was that she wanted a meeting with Dr. Crawford.

This mishap was the coup de grace. I went through the motions of my student teaching until the end of the semester, and then received my pre-arranged "C." This was the deal that had been made behind closed doors between Miss Boltz and Dr. Crawford: Miss Boltz would continue to work with me only with the understanding that I would get no more than a "C" at the end of the semester. Since this was my last class before I was to be drafted into the army in July, I could not drop the class and try again with a new teacher. Also, it was my last chance to be certified as a teacher and, perhaps, avoid the draft with a deferment for teaching in some remote area of Illinois that needed teachers.

But there would be no deferment, since no one was going to hire a new teacher who received a "C" in student teaching. This was very much like getting the mark of Cain. I was *persona non grata* in my frenzy of interviews before my draft date. All the principals seemed to linger on my grade in student teaching – "Sooo, you got a 'C' in student teaching. What was that all about?"

"Well, you see, sir, I was paired up with this crotchety, old teacher – well perhaps 'crotchety' is a bit overstating it. And she didn't like hippies, and I was a hippie. Don't get me wrong – not a drug-taking, protesting, violent hippie, but one who embraced the ideals of change..." Futile. Futile. Futile. It didn't appear Marty Settle was going to ever pick up a piece of chalk in the future. I was doomed to another career, and I had two years to think about it because I was in the army now.

Denouement

It wouldn't take a course in symbolic logic to realize that eventually, I managed to get a position as a high school English teacher, else I wouldn't be writing this book. Ironically, it was my military service that overrode my student teaching grade – the principal that interviewed me was a Korean War veteran and saw me as a brother soldier.

My story with Miss Boltz, though, is not entirely at an end. Within three years of being on the job, I received "The Teacher of the Year" award with a nice spread in the local newspaper, lauding my innovative talents and abilities to inspire students. At the time, I was living in the same city as "The Bolt," and she was still alive and kicking – well maybe not kicking, more like wheeling. I carefully cut out the article in the newspaper and sealed it into an envelope with her address. I included no note, only my return address.

I've always imagined her having tea while she opened the day's mail. Suddenly, after a sip, she spits her tea back into her cup, and gawks at the story's headlines – "Marty Settle Voted Teacher-of-Year." Her initial reaction is anger, but upon second thought she realizes she was wrong about me. She says to herself, "Oh, Marty, how wrong I was about you. Can you forgive me?" Then, she decides to write an Addison essay to apologize for her obtuseness in my case and to give me a heartfelt congratulation.

Of course, no such thing ever occurred, and I never heard a peep out of her. Revenge is seldom as sweet as imagined. Probably closer to the real scenario is that she was having her tea and reading the article. Then she crumpled it decisively next to her crumpets, as her Victorian clock chimed the hour from a different century. She leaned back in repose, for nothing was going to disturb her recollections in tranquility.

Looking back on "The Bolt," I realize that I was much to blame for our catastrophic relationship. I had neither the skills nor the empathy to bridge the gap between the two of us. I was full of changing the world, and she was full of keeping a distant past. In the future after having had more experience under my belt, I realized her beloved Samuel Johnson was right when he said, "He who has so little knowledge of human nature as to seek happiness by changing anything but his own disposition will waste his life in fruitless efforts." Amen to that.

She did teach me that there are sometimes two goods that are rather distant from each other, and they require some valiant efforts to mend the divide. There were other Miss Boltzes and Mr. Boltzes that I taught alongside in my career, whom I not only endured but enjoyed and learned from. This is why I am a great believer in a variety of teaching approaches and a variety of teaching personalities in the profession.

So, Miss Boltz, even though you made a beginning seem like an end, the pain turned out to be well worthwhile. As Joseph Addison would say, "Our real blessings often appear to us in the shape of pains, losses and disappointments; but let us have patience and we soon shall see them in their proper figures."

Chapter 2

Teacher as Subversive

The Postman Rings Twice

As alluded to in Chapter 1, I was a hippie through and through. Being a hippie for me was not drugs, sex, and rock-n-roll, nor did it mean that if you were part of the 60s, you wouldn't remember the 60s. What it meant was that the Eisenhower "happy days" mentality was replaced by a mentality that saw huge cracks in the fabric of our nation. Gaps between whites and blacks, men and women, rich and poor. A hippie was an egalitarian and a person ready to protest for social justice. A hippie was a utopian who dreamed of a new day coming. A hippie questioned all assumptions of Authority.

Going to the army didn't change that mentality in me, but only reinforced my ideals that radical changes were needed in the U.S. generally and in education specifically. Given a second life as a teacher after being in the service, I decided that I would adhere to some of the principles proposed in a seminal work on education published in 1969, *Teaching as a Subversive Activity* by Neil Postman and Charles Weingartner. "The Bolt" incident of Chapter 1 had made me wiser about revealing too much about my philosophies to fellow faculty members and the administration. I needed to be more covert.

My new approach required that I appear outwardly like Clark Kent – conservative dress, haircut, endearingly self-effacing and traditional. The classroom, however, would be my phone booth; the place where once I closed the door, I could reveal myself as the hippie I really was. I planned to change the system not by being outrageous in my class statements but by being surgical in my strikes to the underpinnings of the educational system. I adhered to Henry David Thoreau's "There are a thousand hacking at the branches of evil to one who is striking at the root."

Hoosiers and the Pursuit of the Hirsute

If you've ever seen the movie *Hoosiers*, you will understand the kind of rural community school where I first taught. By 1970, a lot of changes had entered education by way of the liberalities of the time. Not so for this high school in the barrens of corn country. The principal was a throwback to one of those isolated communities in the Ozark hollers. He always referred to the students as STEW-dents, as if we were having them for lunch. It was here I would make my first foray into my secret life of Subversive Settle.

One of the great issues for school administrators and school boards in the 60s was dress code and long hair. What to do with the invasions into schools of "revolutionary" clothing, and unkempt, long hair on males? I had seen principals and vice principals in the past go into apoplexy over a peace sign on a tie-dyed T-shirt or an Afro with a pick in it. Since I had already made my mother cry when I came home from college with long hair and had already been abused by police for my hippie appearance, I had been purged of the absurdity of the dangers of this kind of self-expression. As a teacher, I was of the belief that what students wore had little to do with what kind of people they were or were to become.

This isolated rural high school ignored all the court cases and mandates of the 60s. They had a very strict dress code, which included haircuts for boys. During my first semester as a teacher, a problem similar to the one in *Hoosiers* came to a head – the best basketball player on the team was going to stick to his principles and not play on the team. The community loved basketball more than anything else. They had some strappin' farm boys in the area that always provided competitive seasons for the Spartans. Why on earth was Jamie Davis not going to play? Didn't he know this was a dagger into the heart of the community? The answer was because he wanted long hair, which was not allowed in the system. After many meetings, discussions, and votes, it appeared that neither side was going to budge an inch.

(Enter the subversive who came in from the cold.) After school during this furor, I met with Jamie Davis and told him I had lawyer friends in the city nearby. And that if he and his parents were interested, I could arrange a meeting with them. (I had a feeling that these issues had already been resolved in the Illinois Supreme Court. But it was all a bit obscure).

Old Man Davis, Jamie's father, was a no-nonsense farmer with thousands of acres of bottomland soil and a wallet thick enough to choke a large mule. He met with the lawyers with his tobacco spit can and a fistful of dollars.

He basically listened and then said, "Go get 'em." The next day, the lawyers arrived at school with paperwork in hand to start legal proceedings. The principal was taken by surprise and turned a gobbler red as he clucked around his desk trying to figure out what to do. He called the superintendent, who arrived posthaste. Soon a group of school board members pulled into the parking lot. They powwowed in the office for about two hours as everybody paraded past the large office windows, wondering what the heck was going on. After everyone dispersed, we never heard a peep about what went on from anyone.

It was only on the next morning during class announcements when it was casually mentioned there would no longer be dress or hair codes. The students were stunned, and it took a moment or two before the fuse burned down and they let out an explosive cheer.

In the following months, Jamie went on to grow long hair and to play on a team that competed for the state championship (would that it had ended like it did in *Hoosiers* with a state championship). But I think the most interesting thing of all is there wasn't a damn bit of difference in the students' ability to learn, regardless of what they wore, nor did their behavior turn into defiance of authority. No decadence had seeped in. The sky had refused to fall, and my first act as subversive teacher came successfully to a close.

Boys in the Ban

There are many ways to be surgically subversive, which are quite sound and quite unassailable, if one wants to fain innocence. For instance, teachers in the Jurassic could make their own reading lists. There were few books that were required reading. I would always put together reading lists that, first of all, were multi-cultural before the word *multi-cultural* became popular. I tried to include the voices of women, African Americans, Native Americans, Hispanics, Jews, etc. If a question came up about the use of a certain book, I always made sure I had a justification and not an agenda. Examples would be *The Autobiography of Malcolm X* , which was critically acclaimed in *The New York Times Review of Books* or *Bury My Heart at Wounded Knee*, which had the support of *Time Magazine*'s reviewer, or *The Color Purple,* which had received the Pulitzer Prize.

Another ploy I used was to make mention of facts that were not included in the anthologies of the time. For instance, you will notice in the list I gave above on multi-cultural groups, I did not include homosexuals (the term *gay* had just begun making the rounds in the early 70s). Sexuality was a highly charged area, and it was not until the 80s that I included a book with lesbian scenes as in *The Color Purple.* What I liked to do in this environment, however, was to casually make mention of the number of American literary figures that were homosexuals: Walt Whitman (*Leaves of Grass*); Willa Cather (*O Pioneers!*); Hart Crane (*The Bridge*); James Baldwin (*Go Tell It on the Mountain*), Tennessee Williams (*A Streetcar Named Desire*); and Allen Ginsberg (*Howl*).

Surprisingly, no parent or administrator called me on my book selections, nor did any student seem to object. Occasionally, students wondered how I could know particular writers who had been long dead were gay, and I would tell them how many homosexuals kept their identities secret just as many women like George Eliot used male pen names. And, of course, this was an opportunity for them to do some research. Sadly, I have never had confirmation whether my diversity material had profound effects on my students later in life. This is a frustrating aspect of teaching – that we often do not get to see how our works of art turn out.

Gin and Platonic by the Drum

Readers of Plato's *Republic* are always surprised that artists, musicians, and poets are banned from his utopian society. Yet, upon further thought, it becomes apparent that artists (I'm including all the arts) have a way of getting into the subconscious that are beyond logical thought. Plato was quite aware of this power and censored these activities, which were capable of upsetting societal balances.

Certainly, the music of the 60s had a powerful influence on the changes that were blowin' in the wind. The atavistic return to the tribal drum drowned out the societal values represented by Frank Sinatra. Many of the older generations were disgusted with rock and roll and felt a certain debauchery within its essence. Plato claimed, "A moral citizen's soul will be composed and dignified – but many musical modes stir us up inside and make us jangled and unsettled" [Plato's *Republic* 398e-400d.]. That was good old rock and roll.

As a subversive teacher, I kept feeding my students the pablum of the new music. If they were going to write a paper in class, it wasn't in silence but to the background beats of music they could identify with. I had them study lyrics of songs as poetry – Bob Dylan's, for instance (I agree with the Nobel committee's selection of Bob, as the Nobel Prize winner for literature in 2016).

In the visual arts, I always had posters of contemporary art on the wall, music posters, and movie posters. "Why would anyone consider Jackson Pollock's paintings art?" a student would ask. "I could paint that myself." I never felt obligated to answer that question, but I would point out that the original was in a museum and was worth a lot of money. I was confident that the Pollock had gotten into their subconscious and that someday it would surface in conscious awareness. In one class, I had a student, who liked motorcycles, hang the parts of an entire motorcycle from the ceiling, using fishing tackle, like an Alexander Calder mobile. The parts were always in motion above the students' heads and, once in a while, a student would observe that they came together as a complete motorcycle. The Calder rip-off was as good a way as any to present the feeling of living in a fragmented society that could no longer hold together any one point of view.

I never had one superintendent, principal, board member, or parent object to the art in my room. Some thought it silly; some thought it was my way to be hip with the students; some even thought it was engaging. But none ever found in it seeds of discontent. So much for Plato's warning over 2000 years ago.

On the Road to Damascus

If you have found my subversive role a little offensive up to this point, I quite agree with you. There was a narcissism in believing I could shape the destiny of education by working as a secret agent. It's an attitude that says I know better than you, and I don't really have to defend my ideas in the open market of competing ideas.

This fantasy of mine during the early years of teaching was an adolescent dream of disguised greatness. Pitiful.

Yet, who of us can say that we were not filled with a lot of nonsensical ideas when we were young? Yes, my commitment to hippie ideals was blind, but it was sincere and never cynical. Ultimately, I learned to sift out a lot of the sand from those first years and came to find some pure gold. It is a theme of my life to change reluctantly; as Joseph Campbell states, "the fates lead him who will; him who won't they drag." I mostly have had to be dragged kicking and screaming into new destinies. However, there have been occasions when I have been struck by the rod of enlightenment with a "conversion" that was fairly immediate.

"The soul is to be found in the vicinity of taboo"

As precursors to the hippie period, the Beats of the 50s – Jack Kerouac, Neal Cassady, Allen Ginsberg, Gregory Corso, Lawrence Ferlinghetti, Gary Snyder, William Burroughs, et al. had already established themselves as a bona fide literary movement. They were anthologized in school textbooks of the 70s, and my students had read passages from *On the Road*, *A Coney Island of the Mind*, and *Howl*. These Bohemian hedonists had influenced me profoundly in the 60s, especially Jack Kerouac, but I had never seen any of them up close and personal. Thus, when I heard that Allen Ginsberg – a figure important to both the beat generation and the hippie generation – was coming to read at a university only 50 miles away, I decided I had to go. As a second thought, I decided I would take a few select students with me. What an opportunity to advance their education by having them be in the presence of not only a literary notable but a personality of immense expanse.

Permission was not a problem. The principal had never heard of Allen Ginsberg. So, when I pointed to his name in our anthology, that was all the authority he needed. The note from the parents was, also, easily obtained as I had taken a number of short field trips with students to plays, movies, and local poetry readings. In the end, I had about ten of my best AP seniors crammed into my van on a Wednesday night – all ready to have an adventure at the university.

When we arrived, my students were enthralled by just being at a university. They could see themselves shortly joining the ranks of young adults unencumbered by limpet parents. Eating at the cafeteria for them was like going to a Parisian cafe. I couldn't wait for them to get a real taste of freedom when they saw Ginsberg in all his guru glory.

I intentionally arrived early for the reading, so that we could have seats in the front row. Expectations were high as a group of "heads" set up the microphones and laid out a rug and large pillow. Soon Ginsberg came out barefooted in his regalia of white Indian shirt with beaded necklace and ragged jeans. His hair and beard were as wild as a desert prophet's. I smiled over at my neophytes, and I could see their bodies taking the postures of rapt attention.

Ginsberg settled himself on a pillow before a low microphone. In a lotus position, back straight, he picked up a small wooden box and placed it on his lap. He began pumping a flap on the side of the box and sounds from the Far East drifted over us like incense. This musical instrument was called a harmonium, and it silenced the crowd as they waited for the grizzled poet to speak.

ooooh rongggg - ooh ronga rong - ooooh rongggg
ooooh rongggg - ooh ronga rong - ooooh rongggg
(He was warming up. He was going to recite his poetry to musical accompaniment just like the Beats often did in coffee shops. How cool was that!)

ooooh rongggg - ooh ronga rong - ooooh rongggg
ooooh rongggg - ooh ronga rong - ooooh rongggg
(Pause. Ah, he's ready to chant poetry.)

Suck my d_ _ _ so fine
ooooh rongggg - ooh ronga rong - ooooh rongggg
ooooh rongggg - ooh ronga rong - ooooh rongggg
(Say what!)

ooooh rongggg - ooh ronga rong - ooooh rongggg
ooooh rongggg - ooh ronga rong - ooooh rongggg
Lick my a_ _ so clean
ooooh rongggg - ooh ronga rong - ooooh rongggg
ooooh rongggg - ooh ronga rong - ooooh rongggg
(Wo, wo, whoa there, Allen!)

The blood came to my face with such force that I thought it might exit my pores. I looked neither right nor left for fear that I would make eye contact with one of my students.

ooooh rongggg - ooh ronga rong - ooooh rongggg
ooooh rongggg - ooh ronga rong - ooooh rongggg

Ginsberg continued to spew a dithyramb in praise of sexual acts and satisfactions the likes of which I had never heard in a public forum. Some of these contained both words and acts new to me, which I found amazing, since I had been in the army. As the reading went on, my hopes diminished that he would ever read some of his past poetry. Without the least embarrassment, he went thru the Kama Sutra for gays with unvarying beats from his harmonium. Because we were in the front row, there was no escape without drawing a great deal of attention. And there could be no mishearing – his voice was as clear as an Indian brass bell.

After the "reading" was over, we walked back to the van in complete silence. When everyone was settled in, I turned to them from the driver's seat and delivered a final plea before the jury: "You are aware that if you tell your parents the details of what you saw and heard tonight, I will be sacked. I'm sorry. I had no idea that Ginsberg would get that down and dirty. My fate is in your hands." Then I turned the radio on full blast and drove home.

"The soul is to be found in the vicinity of taboo." One of my favorite quotes from the psychoanalyst Thomas Moore. The key word in this quote is *vicinity*. I had crossed the line with these students and actually introduced them to taboo areas. I knew enough about Ginsberg to know he was radioactive. That exposure to him could be dangerous. Yet I sloppily put together a field trip based more upon my own quest than a developmental understanding of my students. I had done a bad thing. I must plead guilty.

As I'm sure you are aware, none of these students broke the code of silence, or else I would be writing a book about selling real estate. It was a lesson for me that I needed to replace my subversive cape with an adult mantle. My insouciant hippie ways would not wash with these young, freckled minds. It was time for Peter to leave Neverland.

A deeper question arises from this story: what if my students *had* told their parents and school officials about what had happened at the reading, should I have been canned? I ask this because a situation with many parallels to my own occurred in May of 2015. Mr. David Olio was teaching an AP English class in a high school in Connecticut. He was a fine English teacher by all accounts; in fact, he had won a state award for teaching excellence. Near the end of his fateful class, he decided to read "Please Master," a poem one of his students had brought in and one with which he was unfamiliar. The poem was by (guess who?) Allen Ginsberg. The poem was about (guess what?) a sexual act. Are things beginning to sound familiar?

I suppose he read the poem as a filler near the end of class, but this filler turned out to be the end of his career. A student complained; 72 hours later, the district began termination proceedings. A 19-year veteran teacher would become *persona non grata* in high schools across the nation.

For me, this decision was unconscionable. A slap on the wrist might have been in order. This was not a sexual matter like inappropriately touching a student. A good teacher had made a small mistake by reading a questionable selection, and not just any teacher, but an award-winning veteran. I don't believe I know of any teacher who hasn't had a bad day in the classroom and said or did some things that he or she would like to take back. It's a good thing we don't wear body cams. There would be a severe teacher shortage.

In my own case, I think that I could find people to attest to my contributions to the classroom after the Allen Ginsberg Debacle. There are teachable moments for teachers as well as students. A reprimand by the school board would have been much more valuable to me and the school system than having me fired. Sometimes the best in our midst are those who find out accidentally what too far is and get burnt. As William Blake is famous for saying, "The road of excess leads to the palace of wisdom." I know my wisdom Geiger counter jumped another level after the Chernobyl of Allen Ginsberg. Sorry, David Olio, your transgression was lesser than mine; you deserved better.

Wood, Wind, and Water

When I was a child, there was a playground at Washington Elementary School that my friends and I frequented in the summer. Recessed into the bricks of the school were places for inspirational quotations. One quotation that I have never forgotten was "Who dares to teach, must never cease to learn," by John Cotton Dana. That quote expresses something I hold deeply in my life not only as a teacher but also as a person. I was, am, and with luck, shall ever be a learner.

As a subversive teacher, I continued to "feed my head" with my drugs of choice: books, skills, and educational experiences. I spent my summers trying to feed my addiction to wonder. One summer, I went to the Center of the Eye in Aspen, Colorado, to learn photography. Another, I went to San Clemente, California, to build fiberglass geodesic domes and meet Bucky Fuller.

In 1974, I decided that I would take classes at a new university called Sangamon State University. Sangamon

State University first opened in 1970. Part of its charter designated that it be an innovative educational institution. And innovative it was. They brought together the oddest collection of faculty that I have ever seen. There were few traditional qualifications to teach there – having a degree, for instance. With this potpourri of a faculty, they offered a potpourri of courses never before dignified with a place in a college catalog.

As a back-to-the-earther, power-to-the-people person, and environmentalist, I found a curriculum that met my needs as no other college had ever done. I signed up for three of their summer school classes: Wood, Wind, and Water; Homesteading 1; and Organic Gardening. No, I'm not kidding.

The architecture for this experimental college was modern Brutalism, which meant it was concrete, ugly, and soulless (perhaps, I should have seen this as portentous). Having been released from my teaching duties for the summer and dressed in the garb of sandals, torn jeans, and T-shirt with backpack, I barely touched the pavement as I walked to my first class.

Dr. Dave – that's how he wanted to be addressed – told us the first day of class that there would be no syllabus or books for class. We would be learning by hands-on, notes, and discussion. Also, we would no longer be meeting in this room but at his home where we could be more comfortable and at ease. As it turned out during the next few days, I had Dr. Dave for all three of my classes (these were all TBA classes) and all three would be meeting at his home.

As you might expect, Dr. Dave had an old Victorian house with wood floors that hadn't seen a coat of wax since 1900. The windows were screenless and the breezes were partially blocked by thin batik blankets tacked to the lintels. In the living room, there were 10 beanbags in a circle (our desks). A battery of old metal lamps with crystals dangling from the shades provided the necessary light to see in a room with no ceiling light and darkly stained woodwork.

When we arrived for the first real class, Dr. Dave greeted us barefooted and disheveled. Apparently, he had just gotten out of bed. We all sat in an egalitarian circle, and Dr. Dave performed what would be the sacred rite of starting each class: he took out a joint, lit it, took a deep drag, and passed it around the circle. (Again, Sangamon State University was an innovative school.) From there, we began to talk about windmills, water mills, and heating with wood. If you think I had to wait and come later for the other two classes, think again (Sangamon State University was an innovative school). Dr. Dave thought it best to teach all three of his classes at the same time, despite the "authoritarian" rules of scheduling.

During the next six weeks, we had scintillating conversations like this:

Dr. Dave: The environment is really getting dirty, man. We need to change our lifestyles. You notice how I don't use air conditioning. Humans have lived for thousands of years without air conditioning, man. There's no need to condition air if it's in good condition. The Indians didn't need a unit hanging off their teepees, man. Can you imagine a teepee with a unit hanging on the side! (chuckle)

Student: Yeah, like, those people lived with nature. The capitalist fucks only use nature to exploit so they can live in their energy-sucking mansions, man.

Insights like these were so blinding that they made me close my eyes and contemplate (some said I made snoring sounds when I contemplated).

One time, Dr. Dave took us to our homesteading site. The university had an old farm with outbuildings that the homesteading classes were supposed to remodel using the craft skills of the pioneers. The day we were there, we performed the gargantuan task of nailing a new board to an old barn. And since it was hot and we wanted to be one with nature, we spent the rest of the day under a shade tree and smoked another joint.

Organic Gardening was no better. Dr. Dave had a pitiful patch of vegetables in his backyard. He told us he never tainted the soil with pesticides or nutrient additives (or, as far as I could tell, with weeding). He occasionally gave us a taste of something that came from the garden. We were supposed to nod and agree we could taste the difference from the commercially grown produce.

Finally, the big day came, the last day of class and the final exam. We were circled up as usual. This day, we were joined by Dr. Dave's wife, who was breastfeeding. The slurping sounds from the baby added to the general ambience of sipping coffee and sucking on Cokes. Dr. Dave said we needed to look deep into our souls to determine what we had learned from these courses and what kind of grade we deserved. There would no joint today; he wanted the clearest of answers.

"Dr. Dave, like I really learned a lot, you know. You're *real*, man. We gotta get out there and change some shit. You got me thinkin' about Mother Earth, man. I've put in a lot of time thinkin', so I'd be cool with an A."

That got a burp out of baby Dave. The "real" Dr. Dave nodded sagely. "I know what you're sayin', amigo."

The first oral exam was over – it would be difficult to top that. When my turn came for examination, I told him, "Hey, man, I've never taken classes like yours [and hope to never again]. They made me think a lot about my approaches to teaching [I need to tighten up my classes even more]. I won't ever forget you or your classes [I didn't realize how low standards could go for a class or how ridiculous a teacher could be]. I think I deserve an A [Anyone who could endure your classes for six weeks deserves an A and a patch].

If you're wondering why I didn't drop these nonsensical courses, I was going to school under the G.I. Bill and making an additional stipend that the state granted to veterans. To drop these courses would mean no money for Marty that summer, and I needed the money (a lifelong situation for a teacher).

These six weeks showed me how low "rap session" pedagogy could go. Dr. Dave's classes weren't the only classes at the university to use this method. I had plenty of interactions with other students who thought they were doing me a favor by telling me to take other classes whose standards were ridiculously low for the easy grade. My epiphany was that fields of study were called *disciplines* for a reason: they required some hard work.

I had always known the wonder side of education, and I had tried to pass that on to my students. But what I had left out of the equation was the equally important discipline or rigor side of learning. If wonder was the yang of learning, rigor was the mostly dark yin. Competency is one of the most important parts of learning. One needs to feel that he or she is a master of the material. I went into Dr. Dave's class wanting to learn how to make a windmill; instead, I was tilting at them.

Up until the summer of '74, I was a subversive who hid behind a romantic laziness. But I could no longer abide a stress-less pedagogy that had more to do with rigor mortis than rigor. I resolved to add more yin to my classes, be tougher, and demand more from my students. I resolved to demand more from myself if I wanted to call myself a professional in the field. I put away my subversive hero outfit in mothballs in a trunk in the attic. In the future, I would be a team player, sharing the burden of making changes in education and collaborating with my colleagues. I would become a post-hippie.

Only Connect

The fatal flaw in my teacher-as-subversive phase is that in reality I was not connected to my colleagues. I felt a connection to my students, but it was immature. Students really do demand an adult guidance and not a friend along their learning paths. In different manifestations, every generation of teachers has to deal with aspects of the culture that keep him or her from connecting. In my case, I had to work my way through the haze of a romantic 60s. Today, teachers may have to work their way through the dulling edge of accountability and efficiency models of education. Whatever the case, I will end with the epigraph of E.M. Forster's *Howard's End*:

"Only connect."

Chapter 3
The Outsiders

Before J.K. Rowling, there was S.E. Hinton. Her book *The Outsiders* was published in 1967. Since that time, it has sold 14 million copies and continues to sell 500,000 copies a year. Not bad for a first book written by a high school senior. When I was teaching in the 70s and 80s, I would be so bold as to say every high school in the United States had a collection of *The Outsiders*.

Hinton followed up her first book with three more in quick succession – all YA (Young Adult) best sellers, and all made into movies – two by Francis Ford Coppola. The books, in general, had the same formula:

- adolescent brothers in a poor family with missing parents; older brother is a surrogate parent of younger brother, who is the protagonist
- younger brother is a confused innocent with a good heart, but he belongs to a gang or group that has the capacity to get him into trouble
- protagonist hangs with a girl that is upper class; the social distance between them is great

- protagonist gets into trouble and somebody tragically dies or is shot
- protagonist is rescued, does not get the girl, and understands he is loved, and that love can be a tough thing

What has always been amazing to me about this series is how students take to them. They're not particularly well-written or well-plotted, but they touch a chord that resonates with adolescents. The chord may be major or minor, but it tells of teenagers seeing themselves as abandoned by parents, abused Cinderellas living in the ash heap, and outcasts in the heightened drama of trying to fit in as adults in the society.

So, I applaud S.E. Hinton for the comfort that she has provided to many a student looking for catharsis from loneliness and estrangement. In my own case, I remember the small hell that I put myself into during my high school years. Maybe that's why I have always had a special place in my heart for the adolescent outsider.

The Luncheon Club

It started with a desire for peace and quiet. I decided that I would bring my lunch to school, stay in my room during the lunch hour, and forego the chaos of the cafeteria. Perhaps some soothing music in the background. Maybe grade some papers without interruptions or enter a few grades. Take off my shoes, even. But my fantasy crumbled as one by one they found me.

"They" were an odd collection of "outsiders," students who for one reason or another felt harassed by their peers or outside the mainstream of the high school. These students for various reasons found my classroom to be an island of tranquility, where they need not look over their shoulders. Often, my job was just to be there as a benign presence. They did not require my direct attention or instruction. Their dominant impulse was to be left alone.

A couple of these outsiders got lost in chalk. They would draw intricate patterns, cartoons, and swirls of calligraphy on the blackboard for the entire time they were there. Some of these were truly talented, and I stepped back on occasion to admire their creations or humor. My only requirement for them was to clean the board before the next period started. Of course, my chalk supply dwindled quickly – so much so that I was forced to buy chalk in bulk to keep up with their appetites, and I bought a variety of colors to add to their palettes.

Then there was the *Dungeons and Dragons* group. First of all, I had never heard of *Dungeons and Dragons*, which was a tabletop, role-playing, fantasy game (after the Jurassic, D and D was transferred seamlessly to the computer). The game was complex, and the group tried to explain the intricacies of the game to me many times as I watched. But I would always pretend it was too complicated for me and leave them to their businesses without the intrusion of an adult.

What was fascinating about the game was that each player had an avatar with characteristics that he (there were no females that played) created himself. The seriousness with which the players took their avatars and the "reality" they gave to these fantasy adventures stunned me. They would even purchase little figurines of their avatars and carry them like talismans. I wondered at times if it was psychologically healthy to be so absorbed in an alternate universe. But then I remembered my obsession with Zane Grey westerns and how I pictured myself as one of the soft-spoken cowboy heroes in an era with no cowboys. Then, I moved on to more fruitful areas of inquiry.

The witty-repartee group was composed of gay guys and gay/straight girls that saw themselves as unattractive. They loved to sharpen their tongues on the deficiencies of their common enemies in school, including teachers and administrators (I knew that once I was out of hearing range, I was sliced and diced). They were unerringly accurate and unmerciful in their criticisms of others. They were unerringly inaccurate and totally compassionate in the assessment of themselves. This lack of self-knowledge, of course, is the nature of the teenage beast. You wouldn't want to have a jury trial with all teens in the jury. Guilty would be the invariable verdict and death the common sentence.

What I liked about this adolescent Algonquin Round Table is that they were not defenseless. They weren't often picked on because they had barbs and, if cornered, they would use them. They could bring down a bull moose with a well-placed zinger about their victim's physical appearance, social status, or stupidity; a zinger that would make the oppressor the laughingstock of a crowd. Rather than smash them like bugs, one was better off giving them a wide berth and leaving them alone like wasps going about their business.

When I say "gays" were members of this group, I don't mean to say that they were *consciously* gay. They wouldn't come to grips with their sexuality until years later and, considering these Jurassic times, that was probably a denial that shielded them from the pain that they would eventually suffer. Still, many of them had been called "fags" by the macho element in school. I remember one individual who told me years later that he had an epiphany one day after graduating from high school: "It was ironic that all that time I had been called a 'faggot' in school, I really was one."

There were those in The Luncheon Club that were talented but were unable to express their talent. I've already mentioned the chalk artists, but we had a singer in the group that would on occasion stand on my desk and belt out "Tomorrow" from *Annie* and receive appreciative applause, as everyone returned to their activities. Sheila was a frustrated, talented actor/singer with not a lot of outlets. When I directed a musical her senior year, she got her chance on stage and didn't blow it. While the singer was not shy, we had a comic who was. Sharon was an Ellen DeGeneres before there was an Ellen DeGeneres. And, yes, she was gay, although I hadn't picked up on it at the time. She and Sheila liked to talk entertainment and work on routines. Some of Sharon's comedy bits were very funny. I could only listen, however, if I pretended to be working at my desk.

Besides those mentioned above, there was an array of different outcasts that came to my room during noon hour. The sleepers – kids that usually had no supervision by parents and stayed out until the wee hours of the morning – would catch a few z's. "The Walkman Dead" with their audio cassettes, earphones, and heavy metal music from hell. It was as difficult to communicate with them as it was a corpse. A few irregulars, who came in just to see what was going on – they got bored very quickly and seldom returned.

The Luncheon Club only lasted a couple of years. I suppose the vortex that brought them all together ceased upon their graduation. However, during its existence, a couple of defining crises gave me a peek at the seething lava in the fault lines of students' lives. The comedian by the time she reached her senior had become emboldened by her classmates' reception of her humor. So much so, that she became the moderator of a school assembly that was a talent show. Sharon knocked them dead. The audience was holding its sides. Her reputation went from another face in the hallway to Mt. Rushmore. The next day, she attempted suicide.

What! How in the world! This was her moment of triumph. How could it possibly be followed with such a despairing act? The one-word answer: Mom. When Sharon tried to share her pinnacle experience with her mother, her mother denigrated it. She would have no part of a daughter entering into the world of comedy. There was college to attend and the acquisition of a sobering career. Sharon promptly left her mom's babble and went to the medicine cabinet to take all the pills she could get down. Thankfully, her brother found her before it was too late. Mom had no idea of the vulnerability of her daughter nor the earthquake potential of Sharon's sense of self. She thought she was in control with her iron grip when a gentle arm around the shoulder would have been the appropriate response. I think Mom got the point after this extreme form of communication.

One of the chalk artists was a young woman that I had in class from her freshman to senior year. Tammy came from a poor family, which was reflected in her attire. In addition, she was shy and self-consciously overweight. Some students reacted to her as white trash. She would have made a good girlfriend for Ponyboy Curtis of *The Outsiders*. She had an array of talents – funny, smart, theatrical – yet she never did particularly well in school.

First of all, she missed too much school. Her absenteeism kept her from keeping up or finishing assignments. Anytime I called on her in class, she would answer with this affected, high-pitched voice that made her sound like the "dumb blonde" character played by Goldie Hawn in *Laugh-In*. She took her time with the easiest of questions:

Teacher: So, Tammy, is this a run-on sentence?

Tammy: My brain tells me...it isn't running...maybe walking.

Teacher: Running or walking – does this require a period anywhere?

Tammy: My brain tells me...a period would be *nice...required* sounds mean.

As you might expect, I didn't call on Tammy very often, although the class took delight in it when I did.

In her mid-senior year, Tammy dropped out of school to get married, which in itself would have been tragic enough. However, the real bombshell was that she started court proceedings against her father for sexually molesting her and her second to youngest sister. She told me that when her father started to play the same "games" he played with her with her youngest sister, she had had enough.

Suddenly, so much of Tammy's behavior over the years fell into place like an old key that fit into a locked door. Her mother, poor and confused creature that she was, didn't know what to do with the father. All she knew was to gather up the girls and move to her sister's when Daddy came home drunk. The four girls were on the move quite regularly with little time to pack a change of clothing before piling into the car. I hadn't a clue to their distress as I dutifully concerned myself with their absences, missing homework, and grades.

First of all, what Tammy did to her father took a lot of courage and compassion. In the confusion and isolation of her teen years, she managed to address a terrible situation without any adult resources. She had married to get the hell out of her home. And then, she went to a police system that she thought was more likely to harass her than help her and told her story. She would have never done that just for herself – getting away and forgetting would have been enough. No, she decided that she wasn't going to let her youngest sister suffer what she had.

In the midst of all the news and gossip that led up to trial and punishment, I was struck by how much I didn't know about my students. The default mode of most teens is to keep things to themselves. They are not by nature capable of sharing their heavy burdens, seeing themselves and their situations as unique. (I remember my gay brother thinking he was the only gay person on earth.) Denial and secrecy are their *modus operandi*.

When I looked out on my classroom, I began wondering which one of those seemingly fresh faces was carrying a magma chamber beneath the surface. There is more to this profession than passing on knowledge. I told myself: "Walk carefully, Marty boy, so as not to make any life weightier than it already is. And observe, observe,

observe. There are cracks of revelation to be seen by the attentive eye and possible places for intervention."

Here's a short poem I wrote after the Tammy incident to express that creepy feeling I had in retrospect of going about my business without a clue to Tammy's dire situation. It's a fragment of an imagined paper being graded by a competent but clueless English teacher.

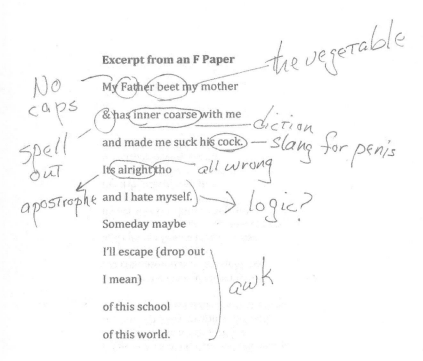

Excerpt from an F Paper

My Father beet my mother
& has inner coarse with me
and made me suck his cock.
Its alright tho
and I hate myself.
Someday maybe
I'll escape (drop out
I mean)
of this school
of this world.

the vegetable

No caps

spell out

apostrophe

diction

slang for penis

all wrong

logic?

awk

Of course, not all members of The Luncheon Club had such tragic stories. But they all were lost in one way or another, and they all were outsiders in the flammable period of life called adolescence. After the club dissolved and the members went into the world like smoke, I could never re-create its magic again. This was an island that arose just once and then sunk again beneath the waves.

On the Cover of the Rolling Stone

The Luncheon Club members were outsiders, but not in some psychopathic way. However, there were other outsiders in my career that were dangerous. And one wondered if they might do something horrific while in school. Columbine was years away, but I read enough student journals and saw enough violent displays, that I worried about how certain students might be tomorrow's headlines.

Nick Rodgers was such a student – nitroglycerin just waiting for a slight shake to explode. He had no supervision whatsoever – a single mom, who was a druggie and just couldn't handle him. He partied all night long, took a variety of drugs, and became street savvy. He'd had his encounters with the police for destruction of property. Once when he was arrested and handcuffed, he kicked out the back window of a squad car.

When I was told he was being assigned to my remedial English class, I protested with all the gusto I could muster. My remedial class had reached the point of being a well-oiled machine, and Rodgers would be a wrench in the works. But the principal had run out of places to put Nick – he'd been kicked out of every English class available. So, in all fairness, it was my turn.

When he arrived at my class with a combative swagger, I paid no attention to it, but did what I'd always done with new, remedial students – I tested him. Without any lecture about what a "bad ass" I could be if he didn't behave, I caught him off guard by methodically giving him a series of reading tests. He was so puzzled by my lack of immediate negativity, that he actually took the tests with genuine effort.

Now, I had no preconceptions on how Nick would do on these tests. After all, he had flunked out of every English class, but that was the result of behavior and not intelligence per se. So, who knew what his aptitudes were? When I looked at the test results, I was shocked to find that he was off the charts. He scored higher than any of my college-bound seniors. When I met with him later, I told him unctuously that he couldn't stay in this class because he was too advanced, and he'd be bored out of his gourd. I could see him begin to smolder. "I knew that I shouldn't have tried on those tests you gave me. I'm not going back to those asshole classes. They treat me like shit." (I ignored the language for the higher purpose of getting rid of him.)

"What would you have me do, Nick? I can't have you here working with students that are ten grades behind you." Again, I felt like Uriah Heep. He had tears in his eyes.

I silently thought, "Not tears, Nick. Any reaction, but not tears. You're a badass, Nick. Badasses don't get teary-eyed. It makes mistreating you all the harder."

But tears it was, and I'm a sucker for tears. So, we continued to talk and, as we talked, I began feeling sorry for the guy. He really was a neglected soul and anger was his response. We finally arrived at a deal. Since he was so advanced, he would work alone in a corner. If he got out of line, I warned him it was back to the "asshole" classes. During our chat, I found out that if he had any positive passion at all in his life, it was his music. So, I proposed to him a daily lesson plan: I would supply him with *Rolling Stone* and *The Village Voice* magazines, and he would write reports to me about his readings. He nodded wordlessly to this arrangement as if it might be just the island of peace he was looking for.

In the faculty lounge, I had a few remarks accompanied by smirks, "How's it going in Mister Rogers' Neighborhood, Marty? Any fights yet?" The emotion buzzards were waiting to feed on my misery. But all I had to say (which disappointed them greatly) was so far, so good. As time went on, it was better than good. Nick came perfunctorily to class every day, read some articles, and did his report. Never a peep out of him. His articles were cogent assessments of music and bands. Occasionally, we talked about what he had learned, and we discussed some of the latest bands. Mostly, I was the learner in these situations. Sometimes, he shared a tape with me.

The only incident I had with him was when he stormed into class one day, turning over a desk and shaking in anger. He was ready to tear the principal apart limb by limb. He was flinging f-bombs in every direction, and there was no talking him down or putting a consoling hand on him. I could see Vesuvius sending up spumes. I said, "Nick, here's a pass. Go to the track and walk around it until you calm down. He was a kinetic kind of guy. He returned a half-hour later, picked up his *Rolling Stone*, and that was that.

Years later, Nick did what all school teachers long for – he called me to tell me that he'd finally turned his life around and wanted to thank me for that year of letting him read about music in my remedial English class. He told me that after high school he went to Houston and within a few years he partied himself to homelessness. One day as he was looking for cigarette butts to smoke in the gutter, he thought to himself it was either suicide or renewal.

After that, he got a job at a record store. Soon he became known to all the bands in the area as a person that knew music and that could promote their records. From there, he became an agent for a number of bands. The voice on the phone sounded strong and confident. I hung up with a glow in Nick's success and in my small participation in it. So often teachers don't get to find out how seeds planted remain dormant for years before they bear fruit in one of their students' lives. It is an act of faith that the deeds done in an obscure classroom in Podunk, U.S.A. can alleviate pain and contribute to someone's successful future. Nick Rodgers confirmed for me that faith.

A Tale of Two Siblings

As I said previously, "observe, observe, observe." And then take strategic actions to obviate failure like an engineer. But sometimes, there's a crack in the structure or a defective O-ring that brings all your efforts to a crashing conclusion. That was how it was with the Huff brothers – outsiders of a lesser god.

I remember the first day of class when I went through the roll and called out the name "Sam Huff." Sam Huff was a big name to be stuck with because it also belonged to a Hall of Fame linebacker who played for the NFL Giants.

Thus, it was ironic when I heard this high-pitched voice and diminutive body respond, "Here."

In the next few weeks, I could tell two things about Sam: he was not going to be a good student; he was going to be a student that I'd enjoy thoroughly. Sam Huff was full of enthusiasm, even though he couldn't care less about what I taught. His passion was nature and being a warrior. About these subjects, he was smart and intelligent. He probably should have been born on the American frontier. Talking to Sam before and after class was learning how to make a rabbit snare, rappelling off a local bridge, or winning a paintball competition.

His brother Jay Huff was another story. Jay should have been the one named "Sam." He was quite a bit larger than Sam, and the students called him "Diesel" because he was built like a Mack Truck. Diesel was anti-social and mean. Everyone left him alone because they were afraid of him. Unlike Sam, Jay had little enthusiasm for anything, except guns and an uncompromising loyalty to his brother. He was a poor student not because he ignored his studies, but because he just wasn't smart. He was a part of my remedial English class.

If you think I'm leading up to talking about them as behavioral problems, you would be wrong. School was basically a place to sleep for Sam, and Jay plodded on with his work if you weren't so rude as to call on him. What was the problem, then? First of all, Sam would write in his journals about slaughter and killing. He was a good artist and illustrated quite well the blood and gore of his entries. Jay would bring weaponry to class – no guns, but the kind of knives James Bowie would feel comfortable with and other skull-crushing paraphernalia like a blackjack and brass knuckles. After I sent them to the counselor, Mr. Remler, he suggested we have a conference with the parents and the principal.

When I got to the arranged meeting, I was surprised to see two women sitting there. Well, I thought, maybe Sam and Jay had gay parents. But quickly, I found that both of them were signing in the silence. After our introductions as translated by the signer, I found out that the father, who couldn't make the meeting, was also deaf.

Communicating with a deaf parent would be a first for me. There's a tendency to look at the motion and listen to the voice of the one signing. I had to keep my focus on the mother and not be distracted by what was happening in my peripheral vision. We laid out to Mrs. Huff our concerns about her sons. Mrs. Huff couldn't have been more pleasant in her interactions with us while at the same time dismissing the fact her sons might have some psychological problems. However, we got her to agree that she needed to talk with Sam and Jay and to try and be more vigilant in their supervision (they had very little).

We had this same meeting with her multiple times in the coming years. Mrs. Huff lived in some romantic cocoon where all was well with her boys and she believed that "boys will be boys." I met the father outside of class a few times, but it was apparent that he was less in charge than his wife. It looked like whatever discipline the boys required would not be provided by Daddy.

These were Pre-Columbine (PC) days, so I couldn't at the time make a comparison between the Huffs and Eric Harris and Dylan Klebold. But looking back, there were overlaps that were quite chilling.

Sam had the cunning, the skills, and the sense of superiority to lay out a plan and carry it out with military precision. He wasn't a psychopath like Eric Harris, but he had his mental problems and was hospitalized in his senior year. Like Harris, he was affable with adults and liked. But, also, like Harris, he was an outsider that had been picked on, and he carried an anger generated by both the school and his parents.

Jay, on the other hand, was a more deeply disturbed person. He didn't really like people and was not the least affable. He would have enjoyed taking out a bunch of people, but like Klebold, he didn't have the intelligence to carry out a strategic attack on the school nor a proclivity to do so. If he were going to do something violent, it would have to be spontaneous. However, also like Klebold, he was a follower and could be led down a troublesome pathway by the right person. Sam would have been the right person.

I had developed a relationship with the boys, especially Sam, who I encouraged to continue his drawing. Occasionally, I took them to the movies – they particularly liked Rambo movies. The only time I ever saw "Diesel" get emotional was during a scene in a Rambo movie, where he stood up and shouted at the screen, "What people call hell, Rambo calls home." Oookay.

But the big influence on their lives came when their parents realized they could no longer handle their sons and sent them to live with their grandmother. How this little gray-haired lady was able to provide these boys with the stability they needed, I can only guess. She was not a disciplinarian or a dominant personality or modern in her viewpoints. She reminded me of many of the great aunts that I had grown up with: no makeup, always in a dress with an apron, had a garden from which she canned, and an old house with worn wooden furniture. Sam and Jay seemed to thrive there like etiolated plants that had been moved into the sunlight.

Therefore, when Sam and Jay graduated from high school, I thought they were on their way to better lives. Soon Sam began to work for an animal rehab organization, and Jay got a job as a janitor for a motel chain. The only bothersome point about their progress was that now that Jay had more money, he could afford to build an arsenal in his room.

Even though Jay seemed to have found an equilibrium in his life, I always thought his engagement with the world was precarious. He was going to need some luck to live to a ripe old age without getting into trouble. But trouble came, and it came in the form of a girlfriend.

"Diesel" had never been in love. From what I've told you about him, I'm sure that you can see that "love" could be a situation fraught with danger. Often enough, being in love can bring out the best and the worst in a man. The zenith of men in love can bring them to new heights of gallantry and commitment. The nadir of men in love can bring them to new lows of jealousy and territoriality. A man like "Diesel" would love a woman uncompromisingly, and he would love her with a focus that could smother her socially. A break-up initiated by the woman was inevitable, and just as inevitable was an exaggerated response by Jay.

Jay took a shotgun to a medical building where his ex-girlfriend worked. People immediately fled when they saw him enter with a shotgun and called in the police. He eventually found his "love" and decided to hold her hostage in one of the rooms. The building became surrounded by police, and negotiators were called in. Hours went by, and they finally managed talking him into releasing the woman. Now it would be Jay against a world that he was never comfortable in.

His brother tried to get permission to talk to him, but the negotiators wouldn't allow it, for what reasons I do not know. There is evidence of some trigger-happy police who put 13 shots in him. There's more evidence that he was committing suicide-by-police. Just like Dally in *The Outsiders*, Jay faced the police with an empty gun.

I have been in contact with Sam over the years and his trajectory of success in the world has been on a steep incline – all the odd behaviors of his high school days have added up to his becoming a director of an animal rehab center. The love of his brother Jay still endures and, when I think of Sam and Jay, I think of the tale of two siblings in Norman Maclean's *A River Runs through It*:

Each one of us here today will at one time in our lives look upon a loved one who is in need and ask the same question: We are willing to help, Lord, but what, if anything, is needed? For it is true we can seldom help those closest to us. Either we don't know what part of ourselves to give or, more often than not, the part we have to give is not wanted. And so, it is those we live with and should know who elude us. But we can still love them – we can love completely without complete understanding.

The Insiders

I don't want to leave the impression in this chapter that I was some kind of Mother Teresa of the teaching profession. While I have helped out a few outsiders along the way and have a special interest and affection for the outsider, I was forced to ignore many in need. Teachers may do some social work, but their main function (and joy) is to have students learn about their field. *In loco parentis* does expand our duties as we become concerned with bullying, behavior, withdrawal, drugs, etc., but there are the constraining factors of how much time we can devote to social work and how much of our own lives that we're willing to sacrifice.

What goes on inside students' heads, or people in general, is a mystery. And it's humbling for teachers to know that certain students are outsiders, and there's not a thing you can do about it. But I leave this chapter with two comforting thoughts: the isolating pain of adolescence is the crucible for the making of a healthy person and builds up more people than it destroys; and that a teacher by just standing by and modeling acceptance can serve in the Miltonian sense – "They also serve who only stand and wait."

Chapter 4
Jurassic Technology and the Blues

Looking to the past and all the technology associated with education – whether it be an inkwell and paper or a clay tablet and stylus – we can see the classroom and the teacher are defined by the equipment that they have available to them (it's hard to assign homework if your medium is clay tablets or you only have one book of its kind).

As a first-grader, I was affected perversely and positively by technology. Perversely, because I was left-handed and had to take a yoga pose in order to write with an ink pen. "Lefties" smeared their ink as they wrote from the culturally biased left to right. Positively, because the later invention of the ballpoint pen had ink that dried quickly and smeared less. Believe it or not, it took teachers awhile to accept the ballpoint because it did not have the flourishes of penmanship that ink pens had. But when it was accepted, I was relieved to discard my crippling pose to write freely.

All new teachers have to learn what technologies are available to them to get a message across and reproduce it. All technologies have secret dimensions, and all are fraught with certain dangers. Before computers and cell phones, I had mastered the nuances of the technologies available to such a degree that if necessary, I could repair them (another possible profession if teaching didn't work out).

Chalk It Up

I fondly remember chalk. The feel of underlining and circling with the spontaneity of a Zen master. The one-hand clacking sound of it on the blackboard tapping out code to young learners. Teachers at one time were intimate with chalk, and all its possibilities. It wouldn't take Sherlock Holmes to determine a person was a teacher from his or her appearance – the telltale dusty thumb and fingertips, the powdered blotches on clothing.

My first couple years of teaching were a matter of learning how to effectively use the chalk technology. One did not automatically know how to write on a chalkboard. I've seen many a newbie write on the board with a painful cursive small enough to challenge the vision of even students in the front row. It took time, but eventually, I developed a board font, which was as readable and appropriate as Verdana on the computer screen. Often, I stepped back in wonder at my blackboard script – reluctant to erase what I had written because I thought it had reached the heights of calligraphy.

A pack of chalk in the old days was currency in the teaching world like a pack of cigarettes was in prison. Teachers hoarded chalk for the day when there would be a shortage (and there always was a shortage). Office supplies were only abundant for a short window at the beginning of each semester, and then they were under lock and key the rest of the time. Secretaries kept a close eye on chalk and made sure there were no disparities in doling it out. If you had a cache of chalk during the lean times, you were King Rat, making all kinds of deals with those who were desperate for white gold. If you couldn't make a deal, then the only course remaining was to keep your nails short, because you were going to be writing on the board with the nubbins – those pieces of chalk that you usually threw away like cigarette butts in times of plenty. These you now gathered and put in a drawer lest they be stolen by an equally hungry colleague.

With these nubbins, I learned a technology could be pushed in all kinds of unique directions. Once when I was writing on the board, Harry Cane almost fell out of his desk when my nails scraped across the blackboard. Apparently, this was a sound that he could not tolerate. Putting this together with the fact that Harry Cane was a rambunctious, discipline problem, I realized like Pavlov I had discovered a stimulus-response sequence that would serve me well. All I had to do to calm Harry down was to make my hand into a claw and threaten to rake my nails across the blackboard. He went from tiger to lamb in a nanosecond. From that point on, I used nails and blackboard as a means of discipline. I'm sorry I did not write this up in a journal of behavioral science and go down in history with Watson and Skinner.

Legends Erased

Accompanying chalk technology was the eraser – the delete key of the blackboard. The eraser had the feel of a shoeshine brush. And it did, indeed, remove all the detritus of the blackboard and return it to a semi-pristine condition. Coaching new teachers, I always instructed them on how to erase and not turn your back to the class; and how to always check the folds of your eraser upon first using it – a favorite prank of students was to stick nubbins of chalk into the folds so that when you tried to erase the board, you ended up with streaks and high-pitched sounds that jarred your teeth. Your exasperation and muttering while you picked out chalk kernels were nourishment to students, who prided themselves in driving new teachers and substitute teachers to insanity.

What many have forgotten, however, is the relationship between eraser technology and discipline. A favorite punishment when I was a child going to school in the 50s and 60s was cleaning erasers, which usually entailed staying after school. One sentenced to cleaning erasers had to go outside and clap the erasers together until there was no chalk dust left on the erasers – and the gods help you if you tried to cheat and clean erasers by clapping them against the school building or on the asphalt playground. Once the erasers were fairly clean (they could never be entirely cleaned), you returned to the classroom covered in chalk dust looking like Lot's wife and were dismissed. This form of punishment was still in effect when I began teaching, and there were occasions when, like a traffic cop needing to fill a quota, I enforced an infraction in order to get my erasers cleaned.

A higher-order skill of the marriage of eraser and punishment was the use of eraser as projectile. There was a long tradition in the teaching profession before I arrived of getting a student's attention or of waking up a student, or of breaking up notes being passed by delivering a well-placed eraser at the perpetrator. I know you're thinking to yourself "How Cruel!" I can only say that it often got the job done without any injury (erasers are soft), except to the psyche, and it got the job done without a lot of stern words and time taken out from a lesson. It was quick, and there *were* rules, such as no hitting in the face.

I still remember the old legends and put them up there with other legendary quarterbacks like Johnny Unitas, Bart Starr, Dan Marino, and Roger Staubach – pocket quarterbacks who could deliver a leather ovoid with unerring accuracy. But as good as these football players were, I don't believe they could have competed with Sam "the Slam" Wakoski, Jimmy "the Tumbler" McConnell, Jake "Sidearm" Wilson, and Bill "the Ambi" Pressler. These guys could throw a cuboid (a much more difficult shape to throw than the ovoid football) with breathtaking accuracy and without pausing during a lecture for even a second while making their throws.

I am proud to say that I witnessed the prowess of these guys when they were at the top of their game. Sam "the Slam" had amazing peripheral vision. He could deliver a strike between the two hands of note-passers without looking their way. A few well-placed hits at the beginning of the semester and students became hesitant to believe they were ever out of Sam's scope of vision. Nobody had such an unorthodox throw as Jimmy "the Tumbler." He liked to hold an eraser at one end and let it tumble toward its target. He was comparable to a knuckleballer in baseball. His erasers seemed to climb up the victim's clothing, leaving spots everywhere. "Sidearm" Jake had the quickest delivery I've ever seen. He needed no wind-up of any kind. He could pick-off a student with just a sidearm flick of the wrist. And last, but not least, "The Ambi." If a student thought he or she had time to prepare for the eraser because Bill had the eraser in the wrong hand, think again. He was ambidextrous and could throw accurately with either hand.

I was pretty good with an eraser, but I was never in the same league as these All-Stars. I've lost track of these guys. Some of them may still be out there. Sam, Jimmy, Jake, and Bill, if you're out there, I want you to know you were the best.

Number 2 Yellow

If there is any icon of education both during my time as a student and as a teacher, it would be the number two yellow pencil. That Claes Oldenburg didn't make a sculpture of one of these pencils or that Andy Warhol didn't include them in a series like his Campbell Soup cans seems to be a missed opportunity on both their parts. How many students of the 1950s started each school year with new, stiff clothes and a multi-purpose pencil box!

This plastic pencil box contained four yellow, unsharpened Ticonderoga pencils. They were cleverly kept in the box by a slide that was a ruler with a sharpener attached to one end. At the beginning of the year, the box glowed like the scrubbed ears of the students returning to school. But by mid-semester, the pristine colors had been sullied by pencil lead smudges, scratches, and cracks in the plastic. Pencil shavings built up in the box like ashes from an incense holder. Indeed, those shavings of red cedar became a kind of incense that to this day can bring me back to second grade.

If you think a pencil is not a technology, try imagining how you would go about making one. The standard pencil with ferrule for the delete eraser should have its place among the greatest inventions of all time. In some ways, it can hold its own against a computer as a writing instrument – it's smaller, more portable. and requires no batteries. Plus, it holds for the English teacher and engineer an illustrious history of being associated with Henry David Thoreau. Thoreau's family made their living by making Thoreau Pencils and, as you would expect, Henry improved their graphite-making process with inventions of his own.

I remember at age seven clumsily holding my number two yellow in hand and tracing my cursive letters onto lined paper designed specifically to help the neophyte learn the proportions of letters. The calligraphy of our culture was well-named cursive and, as a left-hander who smeared everything he wrote, I had many reasons to *curse* both the technology and the right-hander bias.

Today, cursive is becoming a lost art. It was gradually diminishing during my parents' time, as children of my generation had diminished penmanship skills in comparison to the previous generation. My daughter can print but she does not know the swirls and ballet of cursive. She's mostly a keyboard kid. When I began teaching, the pencil and cursive still dominated in the Jurassic, but what is not remembered today is the built-in difficulties they provided for educators.

By the time students made it to high school, they all had developed idiosyncratic kinds of cursive – slanting letters left or right, wild loops, variations of dotting *i*'s, up and down strokes that were indistinguishable from ones with loops, fine-tipped lines and blunt ones, and script that was large and script that required magnification. On top of this, add all the smudges and tears of erasing and smears from hands going over the paper's surface and stains from transporting writing assignments from school to home and back to school again. Now think Rosetta Stone.

As an English teacher, when I got a set of papers from students, my first job was to decode what was written. This doubled the time it took to grade a set of papers. I became familiar with so many styles of writing that I think I could have easily become a handwriting expert for criminal trial work. It was no problem for me if a student didn't put his or her name on a paper. I could identify the author in less than a second based on the handwriting.

Grading spelling was often impossible if it were going to hold up in the court of grades. Let's say a student wanted to be safe about the *i* before *e* except after *c* rule; all he or she need do is to make almost identical short loops beside one another and put a dot between them. Later, the student could claim one loop was an *i* and the other an *e* and that the dot was above the correct letter. Of course, if you just slurred your letters together like signatures from the famous, it was impossible to judge correctness. My response to many students with unreadable handwriting: "From now on, you need to print your papers."

Unfortunately, there will be no movie forthcoming about the Enigma Essays and the men and women who broke their codes. If teachers during this era don't put Alan Turing too high on a pedestal or look down on the "sissy" educators of the computer and printer generation, it's because we are veterans of stronger stuff in an era with lesser equipment and more demands. In your memory, my fellow decoders, I stand up.

The Spirit Duplicator and the Blues

"Copies, I need copies" was the cry of many teachers for centuries. And while the printing press was certainly a major leap in the reproduction of books, it did not make its way into the daily life of teachers. For quick and cheap reproductions of handouts for the class, a rotund, little machine called the ditto machine reigned supreme from the 1950s all the way to the 1970s.

The machine had a little potbelly, which was a stainless-steel drum that went in a circle with a clacking rhythm you could tap dance to. The drum had a slot for the ditto master, and with each rotation a paper shot out, printed in a washed-out, bluish-purple. A flat, plastic container abutted the drum, containing the clear, life-giving, printing fluids dispensed like an IV.

The ditto machine was a sloppy affair, usually entailing blue smudges on the fingertips and streaks along the side of the palm because the ditto master contained a jelled sheet of wax and ink, and handling them inevitably led to stains. Another name for the ditto machine was the "spirit duplicator" because it used a combination of alcohols to coax the ink from the ditto master. You could be blind and make your way to the ditto room because the smell of the volatile alcohol wafted into the corridors. This, too, got on your clothes and became the default deodorant for teachers.

When you ran off a batch of papers from a ditto master (50 copies at most, although I have pushed a master to up to 100 copies), you were left with sheets of paper that were not yet quite dry from having been smeared with this alcohol concoction. Austere was the teacher that did not spend time inhaling the intoxicating results of his or her work. I have never heard about any long-term health problems from sniffing ditto copies or inhaling fumes from the machine. All I know is that students liked to smell them, too, sometimes hovering over a test for minutes at a time before taking it. Maybe it was their gateway drug into the 60s – ditto alcohol to marijuana to cocaine. I always felt a little light-headed after running a series of copies, and teachers at the time joked about the addictive behavior of running unnecessary copies just for the high. We always promised each other that if anyone began to run the machine without a master, we would intervene.

Typing on the two-ply ditto master was a merciless affair. There was no delete mechanism, except scotch tape or scraping with a razor, neither of which worked very well. My dittos were filled with areas I crossed out by hand or typed over. The bluish color of the copies stayed legible for the first 15 copies and then gradually faded into oblivion. It was then that you knew you had to go through the onerous task of re-typing a new spirit master. My class notes and saved material contained scores of dittos that either needed to be retyped or had a few rounds left on the ditto carousel. The used ditto masters ended up getting blue stains on everything. I sometimes come across a few of these old ditto masters in materials that I've saved for over 30 years. They're like purple hearts for when I served in the front lines of teaching. I give them a sniff in an effort to bring back the past, and then I sing, "I got those ditto masters' blues, baby. Those ditto masters' blues."

The Xerox Wars or When No Means Maybe

The Xerox machine, sad to say, had no compelling smell. It did have sounds, but they were symphonic in comparison to the jazz of the spirit duplicator. What was compelling about the Xerox machine was its speed, cleanliness, and efficiency. No dirty spirit masters, just one master copy. Copies looked typed, and one could make unlimited copies as long as the dry ink held out. Further, all you needed to keep for future use is one clean copy. OMG!

Xeroxing did not explode into education like the computer. It was a gradual process by today's standards. Like the first printed books that only the very rich could afford, the Xerox machine was too expensive for the frontline grunts of education. The administration had the first Xerox machines, and we looked longingly as the office machine not only swiftly served up hundreds of pristine copies but COLLATED them as well. OMG!

Intermittent reinforcement, the psychology of the slot machine, is a powerful psychological force. The Xerox machine was a new toy that all of us teachers wanted to make use of. If the administration had said "no" to any use of this super copy machine, the Xerox Wars would never have begun. But we had a principal, who was a generous soul and allowed teachers to use the machine, as long as it did not interfere with any of the work of the administrators. As Oscar Wilde so penetratingly observed, "No good deed goes unpunished." The principal had counted on the rationality and goodwill that would come from his largess. BIG MISTAKE!

In the beginning, the occasional use of the new copy machine was civil. Sometimes it was available; sometimes it was not. Sometimes we were reinforced; sometimes not. But soon there were teachers hanging around the Xerox machine in greater numbers, waiting for a chance to jump in and make a hundred copies. On the surface, we appeared to be indifferent as to who got the privilege of using the machine. If you didn't get to use the new copy machine, you just chuckled and said, "I guess I'll just go sniff some ditto juice." But beneath it all, our competitive juices were bubbling.

Suddenly teachers were arriving earlier to school to copy large collations jobs. Then some skipped their lunchtime to jump in while the secretaries ate. Even staying later after school did not seem so onerous if one had a shot at the goddess of copying. If a teacher walked down the hallway holding a thick stack of xeroxed copies, he or she always had a small smirk for those of us of the blue skin.

Underhandedness of all sorts became the rule of the day. No holds barred – flowers for the secretary, favors for the principal, trumped-up emergencies. The principal, since paper usage had skyrocketed, made a pronouncement that henceforth, faculty would have to use their own paper if they were going to continue to use the Xerox machine. You would think that would have put a stop to the war (teachers aren't paid enough for out-of-pocket expenses). But it did not. Teachers were more than willing to buy reams of paper; and, if not buy paper, then steal paper from the ditto machine or from office supplies.

Thanks to the merciful powers of the universe, the PTA stepped in and bought us our own Xerox machine. The school office then put their Xerox machine strictly off limits. Soon teachers began arriving and staying after school like they had done in the past. The war was over. The only recognizable casualty was a forlorn ditto machine, which had been pushed into a remote corner of the workroom, seldom to be used and never to be loved again.

Jurassic Technology and the Projectosauri

The Jurassic Period of classroom technology is dated c.1950 thru 1990 B.C.E (Before the Computer Era). During this time, a kind of technology that I will call Projectosauri roamed the earth and dominated the means by which teachers projected images on a screen. This species tended to be large and bulky and differed considerably from the compactness of future species that filled their niches.

The *Projectosaurus overhead* was an example of how long in the past it took technology to reach the classroom. It is said that the overhead projector took twenty years to make it from the bowling alley to the classroom. The overhead projector allowed teachers to face the students and write on a transparency with a felt-tipped marker rather than turning their backs to students to write on a chalkboard (Education 101: Avoid turning your back to students; bad things can happen. Such a practical rule was never included but should have been included in my education courses). Of course, you could make a stack of transparencies ahead of time and not even have to erase. The transparencies could be stored and used again, although they did fade out over time. Also, you could be gradually revealing of your bullet points if you covered part of the transparency with a white sheet of paper.

These were advantages that appealed to many teachers, but not to me. I was not able to hold the statuesque pose necessary to stand for long periods next to the overhead projector. I was a kinetic teacher – one constantly on the move. I would tap out messages on the chalkboard, pirouette, and then suddenly be in the back row of class looking at my handiwork and asking questions. I think it was unsettling to students to know that I could be behind them at any moment to see what they were "really" working on.

Perhaps, the greatest loss of the gradual phasing out of overhead projectors was their use at school dances. In the Age of Aquarius, one could make the neatest psychedelic light shows using an overhead projector. All one needed was two clock faces, which were often "borrowed" from classroom clocks, mineral oil, paints both oil-based and water-based (provided by our art courses), and water. There was always a student good at this, and they would make pulsing blobs of colors to go with the music. All I can say for this precursor to PowerPoint – peace, love, and power to the projector.

Projectosaurus opaque was a living fossil that reminded me of the horseshoe crab. It was built like a small, armored tank with a side door to put in the ammo. The ammo was anything that you wanted to project that was opaque – pages from a book or pictures. The picture of Adam and God on the Sistine Chapel could not be made into a transparency at the time nor graphs and pie charts that depended on color. All ye need do with the opaque projector was to open the side door and lay a page flat and "viola" the screen at the front of the room contained one of Tenniel's illustrations from *Alice in Wonderland*.

There were two critical problems with the opaque projector – heat and noise. The opaque projector was more than a warm-blooded saurian – its blood boiled. The cause of this heat intensity was the bulbs you needed to feed the machine (they were constantly burning out). They generated enough heat to warm a classroom in the winter. I often wondered what would happen if I stuck a hamburger in the side door and used it as a charcoal grill. To stand next to the breath of the beast drained a teacher of all energy in about ten minutes.

The other problem with the opaque projector was that its motor was loud. The machine required a rather large fan to dissipate all the heat build-up. Talking over it and trying to make out questions from the class added another layer of annoyance. Mix this drawback with its heat vents, and you can see why even in its heyday, the opaque projector was seldom used. Most of the time it was parked on its electric utility cart in the storage room at the ready to serve. The opaque projector lived a reclusive life.

Everything's Smaller in Texas and Moore's Law

I didn't realize I was confronting the future when an "innocuous" little device from Texas Instruments entered the classroom – the handheld, single-chip calculator. This little device had all the potential that the first shrew-size mammals had during the age of the dinosaur.

The transistor allowed miniaturizations that took us by surprise. Many math teachers were not happy about these small calculators that saved both time and a lot of paper used for hand calculations. Calculators were present before Texas Instruments, but they were large enough to crush a person's skull and could not easily be snuck into a classroom. New technologies are always looked upon with suspicion in education, and somehow using a calculator in math and physics seemed like cheating. According to many teachers, the old ways were best for student minds and, if suddenly they became dependent on calculators, they would lose all sense of math fundamentals. Of course, Socrates said the same thing about memory and the alphabet.

Then too, teachers tend to want students to go through the same kind of basic training that they had to go through in order to learn a discipline. This forms a kind of brotherhood of pain. One of the instruments of pain was the slide rule. A good calculator could put a slide rule out of business. Oh, no! God help us if these calculations became *easy*. What's the mystery! Where's the discipline! The blood, sweat, and tears! Thankfully, my slide rule lies buried in a box in my attic alongside my abacus.

In the mid-70s, there were rumors of how computers would take over society and education. I decided that I would take some cybernetic summer classes at a nearby university to see what the fuss was all about and to determine if computers would be useful in my classes. Most of the computer classes at the time were programming classes, so I took a coding class to learn PL/1.

There were no personal computers during this period, only mainframe computers the size of brontosauri. All of us in class would type up a set of punch cards and then trot over to a large building where they kept the mainframe. We'd feed them to the behemoth, and it would digest a set of cards that we had spent a whole evening to put together in a split second. The results were then regurgitated onto a special printer that took accordion paper. My first interactions with this computer were not friendly. As an associative and metaphorical thinker, I found computer programming mercilessly logical. If I had left out a comma or a word in the programming, the mainframe would spit out a whole sheet with nothing on it but "mistake on line 35" repeated. One reminder would have been enough for me to get the point. But this autistic bully seemed to get joy out of telling me that I made a grammar error and that I deserved to be told about the error fifty times.

I put together six successful coding projects in PL/1 and got an A in the class. I felt confident at this point that I could make some salient prognostications for my fellow teachers:

- The computer was not a technology that would ever make it to high school. Its size alone would require a separate architecture the schools could not afford. In addition, the temperature control factors would be complex and costly.
- Programming might be useful to some of our science and math students, but for the majority of our students, computers would never touch their lives directly.
- Computers are nice to solve huge problems for NASA, the military, and the financial sector, but for the majority of areas in society, computers would have little application.

Thus it was in the summer of 1974, Martin Settle made his ass-tute prognostications about the computer. The little Texas Instruments calculator had not entered into my calculations. I was clueless on the brink of massive technological extinctions and technological redesigns. The new sheriff in town was Gordon Moore, co-founder of Intel, when in 1965 he formulated Moore's Law. Moore's Law states that every year the number of transistors per square inch on integrated circuits will double. Huh? Simply stated, computers were going to get smaller and smaller, while at the same time becoming more efficient. The miniaturizations coming in the future were going to send all the Jurassic technology to the boneyard for future paleontologists to display in the Smithsonian.

It wouldn't be long before my experiences with the early mainframes would make their way into the corners of obscurity. The one poem that I taught about computers in 1974 was "All Watched Over by Machines of Loving Grace" by Richard Brautigan. The poem is about a cybernetic return to Eden where the ecology of nature is kept in balance by computers. Here's a stanza from the poem:

I like to think
(right now, please!)
of a cybernetic forest
filled with pines and electronics
where deer stroll peacefully
past computers
as if they were flowers
with spinning blossoms.

How many today would understand the metaphor of "spinning blossoms," which refers to the large tape reels that early computers had? How long does it take for what many would consider recent to require an asterisk of explanation? Often, I feel like a Neanderthal when I talk about my technological history to the young – "Yes, when I was growing up, we did not have television nor air conditioning. There were people called milkmen who delivered milk to our house." After a brief comment, "Weird. You must be really old," they put their heads down and return to their iPhones.

I guess it won't be long before I'll be wheeled on a cart similar to the stainless steel ones I used for media equipment in the classroom – TVs the size of boulders, movie projectors with metal reels bigger than 33 record albums (if any of you know that size today), videotape cameras and stands that came in cases that would accommodate a tuba. The smart room has blended the functions of all these machines (and more) into a nice compact package. The ubiquitous stainless steel utility carts – pedestals for the gods of media of my generation – all have gone the way of dusty death. Out, out brief projector bulb.

Conclusion: A Whit, A Jot, A Tittle

At this point, I would like to reveal that the first half of my teaching career (the subject of this book) was in high school and that the second half was at UNC Charlotte, where I was a lecturer in the English department. I began at the university just at the time the nozzle of the computer revolution was beginning to open full spray. In that time, I had to endure the humiliating dousing at middle age of transitioning from B.C.E. (Before the Computer Era) to C.E. *DOS for Dummies* was my bible.

Thus, I can say with some authority, having experienced the computer age in its radiant splendor, that I haven't seen student writing improve a whit, a jot, or a tittle with the new technologies. While it is great as a teacher not to have to decode student handwriting, the new, legible lines from the printer or monitor still require thought and imagination – two intangibles that defy any augmentation by computer or printer. Progress is elusive as we move from period to period with gains and losses that seem to balance out. With all the smart room technologies and all the enhancements of group work that computers can bring, there still remains for teachers the unending work of how to get students to put their thoughts into words. Believe me when I say I would not like to return to the old ways. I can't imagine my life any longer without word processing and the internet. But I still think that we must harken back to the words of Euclid and Anthony Trollope, "There is no royal road to learning, no shortcut to the acquirement of any art."

Chapter 5
What Your Education Courses Never Taught You

The Fart-In

The most irritating man that I ever met was the famous labor and community organizer Saul Alinsky. It was no surprise that the business card he carried said "Professional Agitator." In the 60s, he was invited to my college campus. In his first three or four sentences, he managed to insult the people who invited him (the sociology department), the administration and faculty, and the student body. All with a stream of f-bombs, which I had never heard from a public speaker before.

Despite the fact that he was extremely annoying, he was also very engaging. I had read his bible for protesters called *Rules for Radicals*, which was a tome about power. Alinsky was not about ideology but about methodology – how to go about getting what you want by turning the rules of the enemy against her.

A classic example of Alinsky tactics is the suggestion of a "fart-in" in Rochester, NY. Community organizers there were trying to put pressure on Eastman Kodak to hire

African Americans and were having little luck. That's when they called in a "professional agitator." Alinsky suggested that they buy up blocks of tickets to the local symphony performances. Huh? Then, on the night of each performance have a huge bean dinner for those selected to attend. They would carbo-load so that they were prepared to fart loud and long during the quieter parts of the music.

Annoying, yes. Gross, yes. Effective, definitely. Only Alinsky could think up a way to use flatulence as a means to power. And maybe I should add to my opening list – Fun, yes (there were many volunteers for the bean party). Of course, this strategy of farting at concerts was leaked to the press.

What is brilliant about this strategy is that, first of all, the powers that be are the ones who attend the symphony. You don't have to shout or plant bombs to interrupt their fun. Passing gas is not against the law, and to have the participants arrested makes the people in power look silly. Now you can get your concessions without a lot of rational discussions that go nowhere because your opponent holds the Smith and Wesson – or should I say mustard gas.

Although I have never used Saul Alinsky's *Rules for Radicals* for social change, I have used it my teaching career, and I have seen other teachers use tactics that were similar. You will find none of these methods in your education classes or textbooks, and yet, I think, they should be a part of every teacher's survival kit.

Alinsky Rule 3: Wherever possible go outside the experience of the enemy

Kiss of the Spider Woman

One of the deepest fears of a teacher is to suddenly have his or her schedule changed at the last minute. This was the case when I arrived at high school for the first day of classes and was told that the middle school language arts teacher had a heart attack and needed to be replaced. The superintendent called me in for the new assignment. I was to teach high school in the morning and then after lunch, I was to drive to the middle school to teach language arts. "You can't be serious," I said. "I've never taught middle school before, and I know nothing about language arts at that level. I'm highly unsuited and unqualified."

After my reeling, writhing, and arrhythmia, I found myself after lunch saying goodbye to my colleagues (who feigned sadness at my plight but secretly were glad they weren't going to the guillotine) to drive to the middle school. The principal greeted me with all the right phrases of compassion and understanding: "I know how frustrating this must be for you"; "This happened to me once in my career"; "I certainly will give you all the help you need to come up to speed."

After that, we got down to brass tacks about texts, policies, and discipline. Just before I was about to leave to take up my post, he said, "And there's one last thing." I hate that phrase because it's usually followed up with something inauspicious like "Is your life insurance paid up?" or "We've had quite a few teachers leave because of mental illnesses" or "We were forced to double the size of your class."

"Buck Harness."

"Ye-e-e-s."

"He'll be in your class."

"Ye-e-e-s."

"We've had quite a lot of trouble with Buck over the past few years. We've kept him back twice. He really should be in eighth grade. He comes from a tough family. Both of his brothers are in jail. Buck will probably try to challenge you the first day. Have a good first day."

I walked into the corridor like a man that had been sentenced. The bell rang and an explosion of medium-sized middle-schoolers filled the hallways. As I went into my classroom and set up behind the desk, a gray-haired woman bounced through the door. She exuded enthusiasm and bonhomie.

"Hello, I'm Mrs. Garrett, the other language arts teacher. It's so wonderful to have a man on the faculty, especially one that is young and handsome."

"I don't know about handsome," I smiled demurely.

"The children need to be exposed to the male side of things. And I know that you'll bring many fresh and new ideas to the classroom. If you need anything, anything at all, I'm here to help you."

As she was speaking, I looked up as the students were seating themselves. I knew immediately who Buck Harness was. He was a head taller than anyone else with an expression on his face like someone who enjoyed torturing cats. He sat in the middle and broadcasted the fact that he was wearing a hat – an infraction of school policy. His first confrontational move.

"Mrs. Garrett, I do have one immediate concern – Buck Harness. He does look like he wants to challenge me on my first day with his hat on. What would you suggest I do?"

"Oh, don't worry about Buck. I'll take care of Buck." I thought, "You'll take care of Buck, yeah right. An old woman, whose face looks like it should be on a jar of jam, is going to strike terror into the Buckster. Sure."

As the bell rang and the students settled into their desks, Mrs. Garrett proceeded to introduce me to the class.

"Oh, class, it's so wonderful to introduce you to your new teacher, Mr. Settle. Mr. Settle comes from the high school, so he knows a lot about language arts. I know he'll have many wonderful new ideas and projects for you. You should have an exciting year with him.

"And Buck, my Buck. You know how much I love you." Mrs. Garrett, then, walked down the aisle and planted a grandmotherly kiss on Buck's cheek. You could see it was a kiss of genuine affection. Buck's response was to turn the color of a fire truck.

Mrs. Garrett continued, "And Buck, you look so good in that hat that I'll have to kiss you every time I see you in it." The stunned Buck took off his hat and tucked it under his desk, while Mrs. Garrett returned to the front of the room and exited. There was hardly an eye blink from the deflated Buck for the rest of the period.

What I had just witnessed was a master teacher. Mrs. Garrett through the years had attained enlightenment. As a guru, she could only pass on her teaching skills to those in her presence. No textbook could hold what she knew and could do. And what she knew was that Buck Harness could handle being hit, yelled at, punished, and kicked out of class. Buck was familiar with the world of abuse and ready to react accordingly. What he was uncomfortable with was affection. He couldn't be defeated by a fist, but an old lady's lips were more than he could deal with. Saul Alinsky couldn't have done better.

Alinsky Rule 12: The price of a successful attack is a constructive alternative

P.E. Periods

The story above only relates one of my woes upon being assigned to middle school for my afternoon periods. Besides a language arts class, I was to teach a sixth grade P.E. class – a co-ed P.E. no less. To say I was a bit intimidated would be like saying running in Pamplona with a sprained ankle was a bit intimidating. But I was athletic and loved physical activity, so I asked myself "How bad could this be?"

How bad it could be came in the form of a problem that I didn't foresee. After the first week of class, one of the girls came up to me and shyly said, "I can't dress for P.E."

"Did you forget your clothes?"

"No," she replied softy.

"Not feeling well? What seems to be the problem?"

"Well, Mr. Settle, it's my um, er, you know my time..."

"Your time? It's class time, not your time."

"Ya know, my time of the month."

Pause. "Ah, you mean you're having your, ah, period."

"Yes, sir."

This was an area outside my ken. The only periods I knew about were grammatical and class periods. I didn't know what the procedure was for menstruation, and I was sure that such a demure young girl wouldn't lie to me. So, I let her sit out of the class.

As the weeks went on, I found this "problem" grew at an exponential rate. A large number of girls were having their periods and sitting out. Some girls seem to be having their periods quite irregularly on a weekly basis. Yet, what could I do? I couldn't just say, "I don't believe you *really* are having your period" or "Didn't you just have your period last week? I've written it down in this notebook."

One of the pleasures of this middle school was that at the end of the day, a few teachers, the secretary, and I would go out for a beer at the local bistro. It was over a beer that I told them about the problem of the multiplying periods in my P.E. class.

Doris, the secretary, was a no-nonsense, tell it like it is person. "Why those little sons-of-bitches are taking you for a ride, Settle. Can't you see through that?"

"Not really. Surely at such a young age, they wouldn't be lying about something so, so, so...personal as having a period."

"Oh, God, are you a sucker? Of course, they would. These girls aren't fairy tale princesses. They're more cunning than the boys any day, and they'll play you like a trout. You just send them down to me when they try to wangle out of P.E."

So, the next phys-ed class, I told Kim Alexander to see Doris first to get a permission slip to miss class. Five minutes later Kim returned and "whoosh" she ran to the locker room and dressed. Next. Next. And next. All the girls went to see Doris and came back as if they had a sudden conversion to the values of P.E. By the end of the week, it seemed like the girls in class had gone from menstruating to menopause.

When I said, "Go see Doris," the girls seemed to have a sudden change of heart, as if they were just kidding about missing P.E. I never knew what Doris said or did to them; in fact, I never wanted to know because I was sure it was something I could not do as a man. All I knew is that Doris was tough and effective and that she was not a monster because she actually did sign permission slips for some of the girls.

Thus, this niggling problem of periods was solved by giving these "innocent" lovelies an alternative to gym class. They chose the road more traveled by and that made all the difference.

Alinsky Rule 4: Make the enemy live up to their own book of rules

Saul, Saul, Do Not Forsake Me

Not all secretaries that I worked with were as friendly and cooperative as Doris in the story above. There was Lavinia Cutler – rigid both in posture and attitude, officious, and 100% a representative of the administration. In my dealings with Lavinia, I made sure I had all the relevant policies out so I could point to them, and I made sure that I had dotted my i's and crossed my t's. Lavinia loved her little fiefdom of power.

The first time that I called in sick at this new high school, I was surprised how I was grilled by Lavinia. It was like being back in school as a teenager and being grilled by my mother about why I should miss school.

"So, what seems to be the problem, Mr. Settle?"

"I have a runny nose and some congestion in my throat."

"Those don't seem to be serious enough symptoms to miss school. Take a few aspirins..."

"And plenty of rest, right?"

"I was going to say, pseudophed, and come to school. You'd better hurry to make the first bell. Don't be tardy."
click

What the...? I'd never been required to give justification for a sick day at any other school. Lavinia's militant approach of fighting the good fight for the institution was new to me. What was I going to do when I wanted to take a mental health day! Could my story hold up to the interrogation of the Gestapo?

Calling in sick during the first semester was wearying. Lavinia's strategy was working. I began to prefer to come to school sick rather than go through the ordeal of twenty questions. It was time to bring in an unorthodox solution. I cried out, "Saul, Saul, do not forsake me!" And then, my prayers were answered.

First Use of the Strategy
"Hello, Ms. Cutler, this is Mr. Settle. I will not be able to make it to school today. I'm sick."

"So, what seems to be the problem, Mr. Settle?"

"You really don't want to know."

"Please, Mr. Settle, it is my job to know."

"Okay. I have these pustules on my testicles the size of Hershey's Kisses. I'm not quite sure what to do. I think I'm going to soak them in hot water and see if the boils break on their own. If that doesn't work, I'm going to the doctor."
Silence

"Okay, then, I'll call for a substitute."
Second Use of the Strategy

"Hello, Ms. Cutler, this is Mr. Settle. I will not be able to make it to school today. I'm sick."

"So, what seems to be the problem, Mr. Settle?"

"Well, after I took my morning constitution, I looked into the commode and my stool looked like a sea anemone made of writhing worms. They were purplish little fellows. Pretty in an odd sort of way. My dog had something similar in his stool yesterday. Maybe I caught it from him."

Silence

"I'll call for a substitute."

Third Use of the Strategy

"Hello, Ms. Cutler, this is Mr. Settle. I will not be able to make it to school today. I'm sick."

"I'll call for a substitute."

Arma virumque cano, Troiae qui primus ab oris Italiam, fato profugus, Laviniaque venit litora. – Virgil, *Aeneid I*

I sing of war and of a man, who first from the shores of Troy, driven by fate, arrived in Italy, and on Lavinian shores.

Alinsky Rule 1: Power is not only what you have, but what the enemy thinks you have

A Baker's Dozen

In the Jurassic, plagiarism was harder to track down. It wasn't so easy as to type a sentence or two in Google and get proof positive that someone had illicitly used the words of another. Oh, I could pick out cribbed passages easily enough (vocabularies beyond the writer and ideas too sophisticated for the writer), but like in *Law and Order*, it's one thing to know who's committed the crime and another in *proving* that person is guilty.

By temperament and philosophy, I was not a great sleuth in finding out where students had lifted passages. I knew most of them went to the Romulus and Remus of homework help (yeah, right), *Monarch* and *Cliff*, but could not afford to buy all the copies of these that I would need to check out their veracity. Then, too, I was of the opinion that cheating really was a character flaw that could serve in the short term but would not do when a student came up against real competition and real-life situations. It truly was its own punishment in my book.

Then, quite accidentally one summer I came upon a treasure cache. As a reader, English teacher, and person of poverty (Am I being redundant?), I would spend my summers going to garage sales. What better place to pick up books at bare bottom prices – two bits, four bits, six bits, a dollar. With these prices, I could afford to build up a personal library and the library that I maintained in my classroom.

But on this particular morning, I saw in the sunshine glinting like gold ore a box filled with *Cliff Notes*. As I dug around in the box, I found that the substrate was an eight-inch thickness of the red clay of *Monarch Notes*. There must have been over two hundred of them. They included most of the classics, Pulitzer Prize winners, and Nobel Prize winners that I had on my college-bound reading list. Why, who, for what purpose, this particular person had all these study guides, I never found out, but I claimed the box as if the owner were unknowingly selling a Van Gogh. The next school year I would be armed with a new weapon for crime detection.

Every year, I gave my college-bound seniors a reading list of the classics. They were to choose one of the books and then sign up for a book report. They could not sign up for a book that someone else had chosen; it was first come, first serve. Most chose books very carefully based on...you've got it...size: *The Old Man and the Sea* and *Animal Farm* were in great demand. These book reports were due every three weeks and, as you might expect, many fell behind in their reading and resorted to illegal shortcuts.

Since I now had all those study guides, when I graded my first two sets of AP papers, I could easily go to my treasure box and check out suspicious passages. I caught six students red-handed, or should I say read-handed. Not a bad day's work, but I was still bothered that there were plenty of other papers that were questionable, but not provable. What to do? And then, I had an Alinsky moment.

When it came time to hand back the papers, I told the class that while all the papers had A's on them (I always gave A's to people who fulfilled the assignment in a reasonable way), I was sad to say that some had plagiarized. In my grade book, I had entered an F for these people. However, it would make me feel much better about the cheaters if they would come and apologize to me and promise in the future to avoid plagiarism.

How this worked on the minds of achieving, super ego, college-bound students was amazing. They couldn't stand the idea that they had been caught, and that I would think less of them. I had played my cards right and they had gone for the bluff. While I had caught six plagiarizers fair and square, thirteen confessed. I had to return to my grade book, erase seven A's and replace them with F's. Not a bad day's work. Of course, this ploy became part of my arsenal of tricks for the future.

Side Note: A Hard Rain Gonna Fall

As I was writing this chapter, Bob Dylan had given his Nobel Prize acceptance speech, a required exercise if he was going to claim the prize. I was quite surprised at the committee's selection of Dylan for the Nobel Prize for Literature, but the more I thought about it, I realized it was a brilliant decision. Indeed, the minstrels of yore were often the poets of their times. Bob's lyrics spoke to me in the 60s, and he captured the period like no one else with his songs being the chilling winds of the times.

But then, after initial praise for his acceptance speech, he was accused of plagiarizing a significant part of his speech. Some defended Bob Dylan with the idea that the times are a-changin' with regard to what is considered plagiarism. That actually the internet is a place for intermixing of materials that nobody owns – it's communal. That sounded more like lawyerly sophistry than a substantial defense.

I knew as a teacher from the Jurassic, I would have given Bobby Zimmerman an F in my class for paraphrasing too closely *Spark Notes*. And I would have given him *my* speech that cheaters never win for long. (I can hear your laughter at this point, dear reader.)

When I think about the absolute beauty and profundity of William Faulkner's acceptance speech and then think about Dylan's not being able to come up with something original for his speech, you can bet yurassic that it makes me ill. *Spark Notes*! How absolutely pitiful from a Nobel Prize winner for literature!

"Fart Proudly"

To be a devotee of Alinsky, you often have to, like Goldsmith's play, stoop to conquer. Saul Alinsky was not the first American to be able to use farts to his advantage. Benjamin Franklin's famous essay "Fart Proudly" indicates a bawdy sense of humor to make a point. The essay was written in response to a call for scientific papers by the British Royal Society. Franklin believed that many of the proposals for the scientific papers of his time had reached the level of absurdity (a problem that continues to exist in academia).

By "seriously" proposing the study of how to make farts more acceptable in social situations, Franklin had set a precedent spanning two hundred years to Saul Alinsky. Interestingly enough, Benjamin Franklin had his rules like Alinsky. His rules were called "Rules on Making Oneself Disagreeable." If Alinsky hadn't read them, I'd be surprised.

In conclusion, when all else failed in solving problems in my career, I thought long and loud about the tradition of farts and Saul Alinsky. There are many non-violent, moral, legal, and fun ways to get what you want. Here are Alinsky's rules, and keep in mind that it may require some inde-scent behavior on your part. Pew can be more effective than coup at times:

The 13 Rules for Radicals

1. Power is not only what you have, but what the enemy thinks you have.
2. Never go outside the experience of your people.
3. Wherever possible go outside the experience of the enemy.

4. Make the enemy live up to their own book of rules.
5. Ridicule is man's most potent weapon.
6. A good tactic is one your people enjoy.
7. A tactic that drags on too long becomes a drag.
8. Keep the pressure on.
9. The threat is usually more terrifying than the thing itself.
10. The major premise for tactics is the deployment of operations that will maintain a constant pressure on the opposition.
11. If you push a negative hard enough, it will break through into its counterside.
12. The price of a successful attack is a constructive alternative.
13. Pick the target, freeze it, personalize it and polarize it.

Chapter 6
Taking Humor Seriously

Seriously, folks (the old standup comedian phrase), I agree with Robertson Davies when he says, "The love of truth lies at the root of much humor." We all know it is a necessity in the classroom as well as in daily life. Humor is the grease that keeps the social engine from seizing up. Yet despite its importance, it is mostly looked down upon as a means to the truth; it is not included as a subject in the curriculum for students preparing to be teachers.

The hidden assumptions are: 1. that you can't be a serious educator if you're funny; 2. you're taking unnecessary risks in offending somebody or some group; 3. laughter emanating from your classroom is a sure sign that you're losing control of your class; 4. it's a waste of time to make the effort to add humor to your lesson plans.

Marshall McLuhan, the Canadian guru of the 60s, once said "Art is anything that you can get away with." If I might add a corollary to this dictum, I would say, "Humor is anything that you can get away with." Humor always toes the line between what is acceptable and unacceptable. Make a wrong move, and you're into the area of taboo. If you want to know the values and attitudes of a culture, look to its humor, and you can find an objective answer.

I tried to use the acceptable humor of the Jurassic, and I'm sure there was a time or two I overstepped the boundaries. But, for many reasons, which I will elucidate below, I found humor a means to get at things that were difficult to arrive at by any other means. It was a conscious decision on my part to include a category in my lesson plans called "humor." The question for me was how could I integrate the humorous somewhere in the writing exercises and topics of discussion? I found humor to be an important element in my teaching, and I had few restrictions from Jurassic parents or administrators from using it, which may not be the case today.

Revision: A Modest Proposal

It's very difficult to write satire today in an era of the internet and fake news. I've had college students hand me papers with *The Onion* as their news source. Satire can only be satire if recognized as such. I'm afraid the modern response to Swift's "A Modest Proposal" would be that it was a serious proposal to curb world population while at the same time feeding the hungry.

Yet I have found that I have reveled in the truths that have come to light under the magnification of satire. Mike Royko and Art Buchwald were my mentors during the Vietnam years and thereafter. If you wanted to find me on most mornings in college, it would be in the cafeteria with a Styrofoam cup of coffee and two newspapers: *The Chicago Daily News* and *The Washington Post*. I fed on the meat of Royko's making an ass of Chicago's mayor, "Dirty Dick Daley," last of the city bosses. Art Buchwald, on the other hand, had larger pastures of asses to satirize with the bumbling politicians in Washington, D.C.

I've tried to pass on to my students their wisdom, which in a nutshell is: the best way to argue may not be to be logical and formal but to be absurd and ridiculous. The example I gave to my college-bound students was close to their hearts – the college application letter. All of them had or would be writing that essay to college admissions stating their college goals and why they wanted to go to college. As an example, I would give them the following essay written by Hugh Gallagher:

ESSAY: IN ORDER FOR THE ADMISSIONS STAFF OF OUR COLLEGE TO GET TO KNOW YOU, THE APPLICANT, BETTER, WE ASK THAT YOU ANSWER THE FOLLOWING QUESTION:

ARE THERE ANY SIGNIFICANT EXPERIENCES YOU HAVE HAD, OR ACCOMPLISHMENTS YOU HAVE REALIZED, THAT HAVE HELPED TO DEFINE YOU AS A PERSON?

I am a dynamic figure, often seen scaling walls and crushing ice. I have been known to remodel train stations on my lunch breaks, making them more efficient in the area of heat retention. I translate ethnic slurs for Cuban refugees, I write award-winning operas, I manage time efficiently. Occasionally, I tread water for three days in a row.

I woo women with my sensuous and godlike trombone playing, I can pilot bicycles up severe inclines with unflagging speed, and I cook Thirty-Minute Brownies in twenty minutes. I am an expert in stucco, a veteran in love, and an outlaw in Peru.

Using only a hoe and a large glass of water, I once single-handedly defended a small village in the Amazon Basin from a horde of ferocious army ants. I play bluegrass cello, I was scouted by the Mets, I am the subject of numerous documentaries. When I'm bored, I build large suspension bridges in my yard. I enjoy urban hang gliding. On Wednesdays, after school, I repair electrical appliances free of charge.

I am an abstract artist, a concrete analyst, and a ruthless bookie. Critics worldwide swoon over my original line of corduroy evening wear. I don't perspire. I am a private citizen, yet I receive fan mail. I have been caller number nine and have won the weekend passes. Last summer I toured New Jersey with a traveling centrifugal-force demonstration. I bat 400. My deft floral arrangements have earned me fame in international botany circles. Children trust me.

I can hurl tennis rackets at small moving objects with deadly accuracy. I once read Paradise Lost, Moby Dick, and David Copperfield in one day and still had time to refurbish an entire dining room that evening. I know the exact location of every food item in the supermarket. I have performed several covert operations for the CIA. I sleep once a week; when I do sleep, I sleep in a chair. While on vacation in Canada, I successfully negotiated with a group of terrorists who had seized a small bakery. The laws of physics do not apply to me.

I balance, I weave, I dodge, I frolic, and my bills are all paid. On weekends, to let off steam, I participate in full-contact origami. Years ago, I discovered the meaning of life *but forgot to write it down. I have made extraordinary four-course meals using only a mouli and a toaster oven. I breed prizewinning clams. I have won bullfights in San Juan, cliff-diving competitions in Sri Lanka, and spelling bees at the Kremlin. I have played Hamlet, I have performed open-heart surgery, and I have spoken with Elvis.*

But I have not yet gone to college.

When I read this letter aloud in class, it was always good for few laughs. But then I asked, "Seriously, folks, was this an effective letter?" This was where I slipped easily into the writing strategy of audience analysis. At the heart of the very best writing I told my students is revision (not editing). Most of my students (most writers, for that matter) want to be done after the first draft and move to a final edit (correcting spelling and grammar). It's the Kentucky basketball approach to writing: one and done. Editing, I told them, is not revision. Revision is going back to your initial draft and being willing to change it radically.

If your knee is not bouncing up and down under your desk because you'd like to be finished but know you are not, you are at the first stage of revision. Revision is hard, the hardest part of good writing. The question becomes, "What can I do to re-vision my draft?" The answer: write the next draft after an audience analysis. Write for the reader and not yourself.

What does the college admission person do when he or she has to read a thousand application letters that are serious, formal, and unoriginal, and then across his or her desk comes Hugh Gallagher's letter? Most thought she'd be relieved to laugh and give him a pass for his unique approach and sense of humor. Could the college application letter use some satirizing? I thought my students felt like it was a meaningless hoop that they had to jump through and that it was more an exercise in fiction than any kind of insightful self-analysis. But whatever students concluded, they saw how radically an essay could be changed if they thought about the person who was going to read it, and that was the point of the exercise. Satire was a salient way to show what a different approach to an audience can mean.

When it came time for me to advise my daughter to write such a letter, I put my faith into what I had taught over the years and coached her into changing her first draft into a humorous essay rather than a blah-blah essay about how great her aspirations were. Whether her letter was a turning point, I don't know, but she did get into two difficult schools in North Carolina (where we live): UNC Chapel Hill and Wake Forest. I modestly rest my proposal for using satire as a revision strategy.

Note: Hugh Gallagher used the above essay first in a writing contest. Later he claims to have used it for college admission. Whatever the case, I still found it effective for my purposes.

Humor as a Probe

If you are a proponent of writing as thinking as I am, you will be interested in ways to show your high schoolers the hidden assumptions that they make as members of a culture. It always makes for richer writing, if the writer can break outside of cliché and into some real insight. Until the teenage years, culture is accepted as a given; its existence is as invisible as water is to a fish. Once a student enters high school, she or he is ripe to begin peeking above the water's surface and seeing a puzzling shore.

One of the approaches that I used to nurture this awareness of culture was jokes. I told my class that we were going to get scientific with jokes. We were going to lay them out on a dissecting table and closely scrutinize their anatomy. Of course, on the way to understanding jokes, we told jokes, which always added to the atmosphere of the class.

The Light Bulbs Go on

Light bulb jokes were in vogue during one of my stints of teaching. So, I decided to use examples from this genre for my cadavers. If you don't know light bulb jokes, here are a few examples:

Q. How many **psychologists** does it take to change a light bulb?

A. One, if the bulb is willing to change.

Q. How many **used car salesmen** does it take to screw in a light bulb?

A. One seems kind of low. I'll have to check with my manager.

Q. How many **husbands** does it take to screw in a light bulb?

A. One – but then he plays golf the rest of the weekend.

It required very little at the beginning of this exercise to reveal the basic anatomy of this kind of joke: 1. the question part of the joke selected a group to make fun of; 2. the statement part of the joke used a generalization about that group. Here's the joke that I started to get serious about and, I believe, was the original joke that got the light bulb genre going.

Q. How many **Pollacks** does it take to screw in a light bulb?
A. Three. One to hold the bulb and two to turn the ladder.

Who is the group and what is the assumption? Answer: Polish people and Polish people are stupid. Once these were answered, we began to delve deeper into the use of "Pollack." This was a good place to talk about synonyms and connotation. I told them there are no true synonyms – words for the same group or thing that equate one to one. As an example of this, I go through an exercise that S.I. Hayakawa introduced me to: Conjugation of an irregular verb.

I am **hefty** | you are **overweight** | he or she is **fat**
I am **mellow** | you are **tipsy** | he or she is **drunk**
I am a **gentleman** | you are **effeminate** | he is a **faggot**
I am a **playboy** | you are a **hustler** | she is a **slut**

The exercise makes one aware that we use different words when we describe ourselves (I), those we are face-to-face with (You), and those at a distance (He, She, or They). We save the best connotations for ourselves and the worst for those at a distance. The last two examples get us into sexuality and feminism issues.

So, we begin to transplant other words for the groups in the jokes. Jews, for instance. How many Jews does it take to change a light bulb? What are the connotations here? Does "Jew" have negative connotations, or should we use Jewish? Afro-Americans (a recent label at that time) versus Negro versus Black versus worse. There's a lot to be discussed here.

If we then move to the second portion of the light bulb jokes, we get into the hidden assumptions of stereotype – is it true Polish people are stupid? Where did this come from? Why do we feel comfortable using this group for stupidity? Is there a stupid group of people? Can we test them to get some "objectivity" on the subject?

At this point, I gave them the BITCH – Black Intelligence Test of Cultural Homogeneity. In 1972, Robert Williams developed an intelligence test that used material from black ghettos for questions. Black teens from the ghetto did rather well on the test, while students not from the ghetto culture (including black teens) didn't do very well. Since I didn't have any students from the ghetto, my students did rather poorly. Of course, they complained that their humiliating scores were a result of bias. And I agreed, but then I asked if IQ tests, in general, could be culturally biased? The discussion was enlight-bulbing.

Using jokes turned out to be an excellent way to teach students to become aware of cultural bias, stereotypes, and hidden assumptions. As Marshall McLuhan pointed out, humor is a probe. You can always find out the climate of a culture by seeing what people laugh at and what they don't find funny. With a little bit of fun with jokes, I feel like I was able to make visible for many students the all-pervasiveness of their culture. Once this door was open, I could demand more thinking on writing assignments that had to do with the issues of the time.

On a concluding note, dear Reader, I have saved a few light-bulb jokes just for you. You can decide the stereotypes and hidden assumptions that each one of them makes.

Not wanting to leave myself and my profession out of the equation –

Q. How many **English teachers** does it take to change a light bulb?

A. So that's why it's dark in here!

My favorite light bulb joke that I couldn't use in class –

Q. How many **New Yorkers** does it take to change a light bulb?

A. None of your fockin' business.

Here's one of my own creations that I found amusing, but no one else seems to. It's a Pollock joke.

Q. How many **Jackson Pollocks** does it take to change a light bulb?

A. I don't know, but a child could do it. (Rim shot)

Seriously, folks, I'm through here.

Embracing Your Inner Fool

Not all humor enters the classroom as planned; there are always opportunities for a teacher to play the fool. If you think that I am saying I accepted foolishness in the classroom, you would be wrong. I am saying that I *embraced* it. I embraced it in accordance with Marshall McLuhan's insight that "When people become too intense, too serious, they will have trouble in relating to any sort of social game or norm."

Shakespeare knew this well, as he wrote many a scene with drunkards and fools being introduced precisely at the right time to keep a tragedy from becoming too morose. Humans cannot live by bread alone nor by the high carb diet of learning without comic relief.

Thus, you have a choice when you're caught up in an embarrassing moment: you can turn red, shush the class, and become angry if the laughter continues; or you can laugh *with* others good-naturedly as they laugh *at* you. Below are a few examples of when I was forced to wear motley.

1. Harlequin and Handstands

In my youth, I was nimble and physically agile. One of the feats that I had a reputation for when I was in high school was being able to do handstands and walk on my hands. This was an ability that I cultivated and practiced until I turned 60, when I gave it up for fear of hurting my back.

Doing handstands fits in well with the old harlequin roles. The early harlequins in plays, besides wearing their checkered outfits, were always agile both physically and mentally. This role appealed to me, and occasionally I'd do a handstand for my class on my desk to break the monotony. It became a tradition for my new classes to request my doing a handstand on the desk. I'd always put them off until the time was ripe for some comic relief.

Of course, part of all this was being a bit of a show-off and, as is the way of all show-offs, you eventually make a real fool of yourself. When the time came for the mandatory handstand-on-the-desk routine, I took a short run to the desk and went up into a perfect handstand. The line between my head and toes was straight, and I did not waiver for a second to establish my balance. (In the parlance of gymnastics, I *stuck it*.) This emboldened me to go farther because I felt that today I could do no wrong. I decided to come down ever so slowly to the bent press position where my elbows rested on my knees. And I executed this perfectly, ending with the rrrrrripping sound of the back of my pants splitting from belt to crotch.

In that heightened moment of embarrassment, I continued the routine with a dismount from the desk quickly turning my backside from the class. Even though the class was in hysterics, I must say that my dismount was something to behold for its agility and quickness. I raised my arms as if at the end of a difficult gymnastic routine, maintained a serious expression, and then bowed. This was followed by my own laughter as I collapsed in the chair behind my desk from which I conducted the rest of the class.

Lucky for me, a coach had a spare pair of sweatpants and the home economics teacher had a few spare moments to sew me up. The next day's school announcements included a plea for donations for the Larger Pants for Mr. Settle Drive. I had made an ass of myself both literally and figuratively. And I became a humbler butt-wiser man.

2. *Never Let the Left Foot Know What the Right Foot Is Doing*

Anne Puchard was a student that thought I was not only absolutely useless to her life but also to the world in general. Now I had many students that thought I was useless to their lives and didn't give a damn about what I was teaching, but all of them at least thought I had a function in the world, as remote as it was from their interests.

Not so with Anne Puchard. She wasn't a troublemaker in class. She sat passively in her seat as if she were on a bus looking out the window. She found class time a good time to file her nails and chew gum contrapuntally. She was biding her time as a senior, and she knew exactly what she wanted from life – she would go to beauty school and work in a salon; she would find a handsome husband to be beautiful with her. None of her goals included anything from me whether from reading, writing, or personality.

First of all, I was not beautiful or handsome. I think she could have tolerated me if I had any kind of features that were handsome. Secondly, I wasn't stylish, and she was into the latest fashion statement for both men and women. Anne Puchard was always impeccably coiffed. Her hair was perfection, as were her make-up, nails, and clothing. As an English teacher into the "higher" beauties of life, I never took much of an interest in my attire, which put me very low in her estimation of my worth.

As I did with all my students, I asked questions about the work we were doing in class. I never knew what kind of answer that I would get with Anne, but I knew it would never be relevant to what we were doing in class. When I called on her, she would look up from her emery board with a sigh.

"Anne, what is the gerund in sentence five?"

"What page is that on again?" she would ask in a kind of gun moll voice. Then would follow a flipping of pages and a long colorful nail tracing the sentence.

"A gerund, did you say? Is that an animal?" (class tittering)

"No, dear, it's a colon disease."

"Ewwww!"

Oh, well, I had tried, but she always brought out a degree of disgust in me – probably a resentment on my part that I couldn't touch her with anything I had to say.

As a sensitive husband, when I arose earlier than my wife to dress for school, I never turned on the lights, so that she could get those extra z's before embarking on her career as a social worker. This particular morning was no different than any other. I arrived at school with a Styrofoam coffee cup in hand, and I gradually went over the lesson plans for the day and ran off tests and worksheets. Nothing seemed very different to me, nor to any of my colleagues or students.

Then came third period, the period I had Anne, queen of always directing her attention to the inappropriate focus. I stood in front of the class and began our morning activity when Anne shrieked, "Oh, my god! He can't even dress himself. Look, Mr. Settle has on two different shoes!"

I looked down; sure enough, in the darkness of my bedroom, I had accidentally slipped on two different shoes. They didn't feel any different. I hadn't paid any attention even when driving to school nor did my colleagues or my first and second-period classes notice. But, alas, the person that thought I was an idiot noticed, and now she had incontrovertible evidence that I was, indeed, an idiot.

At first, I tried to explain, but then said to myself – "What the hell. Sartorial splendor was not one of my strong suits, and I may as well humbly acknowledge my hopelessness in the area." For the next couple of weeks, I wore unmatched shoes to further underline my inability to cope with the daily routine of dressing for school. In my honor during senior week, the student council proclaimed an unmatched-shoe day. Of course, I wore shoes that matched that day, not to be caught conforming with any style.

3. Zip Codes, a Final Warning with Satire

Many do not realize the origin of the full podium came concomitantly with the invention of the zipper for men's pants. I always requested a podium with an empty shell beneath. Some thought it was because I wanted to separate myself from my students, some thought it was to hide behind, and some thought it was an organizational tool for my notes. But actually, it was to soften the blow of a foolishness common to men.

My podium usually stood a ways from the side of my desk. I really didn't use it that often because I liked to circulate around the classroom. However, when I noticed that I had said nothing amusing, and there were a host of unaccountable smiles from those "pure" faces seeking learning, I knew it was podium time.

It was then I made my way without hesitation in my speech or actions to stand quite naturally behind the podium. Once there with the hand that was not gesticulating, I made a surreptitious zipper check. As was often the case, my zipper was down and its teeth smiling. You can be assured that no one in the class was going to tell me that my zipper was down and spoil the fun. After I zipped up (again with the highest degree of discretion), I walked out behind the podium with a new authority and looked out upon a lot of disappointed faces.

I contend that this gender "zipper" issue that is so seldom encroached upon in the educational journals should be given voice. So, I am picking up the gauntlet and forewarning all new male teachers that there are ways to avoid this inevitable embarrassment and that, perhaps, to be absolutely prepared they might invest in a personal podium.

Conclusion: What are ya doin', Marshall McLuhan?

Q. How many feminists does it take to change a light bulb?
A. One and there's nothing funny about it.

If you do an analysis of this joke, you might conclude that the PC environment of today has killed a lot of humor. And, indeed, it has. As a child of a family that ran a restaurant and bar in the 50s and 60s, I knew the jokes of the day inside and out. One of the reasons for my popularity in grade school and high school was I was on the cutting edge of the current jokes I had heard at the bar. I passed on these jokes with gusto and enthusiasm, not realizing that "cutting edge" could be used with a double meaning for the groups I made fun of.

One of the few advantages of growing old is that you can compare the past and present. I have intimately known pre-PC humor, and I know today's humor within the PC environment. Let me say unequivocally that I will take any day the excesses of PC over the excesses of the unrestricted freedoms of pre-PC. That said, I do believe that many teachers shy away from being humorous in the classroom today for fear that one slip-up will cost them their job. Sad. (I refer you to Mr. David Olio's story in my chapter called "Teacher as Subversive.")

I really question whether my Jurassic humor would make it in today's educational system. What I don't question is the essential nature of humor in the classroom. "Our time presents a unique opportunity for learning by means of humor – a perceptive or incisive joke can be more meaningful than platitudes lying between two covers." You're still relevant today, Marshall McLuhan.

Chapter 7
Prankenstein

"Without a story, there is no community" – this quote (I have never been able to find its source) has always penetrated deeply into my abiding belief in the power of the story. It became part of my philosophy in the classroom to try to create a special story with each class. Once a story becomes injected into the dynamics of a class, many things become easier: work becomes more lighthearted; there's an increased willingness to seek answers and ask questions; discipline becomes more consensual.

The question becomes – how does one go about making a class go from being a collective to a community? Something has to happen in class beyond the routine; some incident, accident, or scheme that becomes memorable. One of the ways among many that I found effective to create a bonding story is the lowly prank, a word like *pun* that gets a bad rap but has its higher purposes. I know many people don't like pranks because they can be cruel and sadistic. I always tried to make mine mischievous and to never walk over the boundary into the hurtful.

Most of us remember the movie *The Sting* with Paul Newman, Robert Redford, and the wonderful ragtime music of Scott Joplin. The following pranks reach nowhere near the heights of the sting operation in this movie. But while not as complex, I found these pranks added a little spice to the daily fare of the school day and created stories that were told at school reunions years after.

Principles from the Principal

Over the years, I've worked with many principals. Sad to say, I never worked with a principal that was truly an educator – administrators, yes; disciplinarians, yes; liaisons, yes – but intellectuals of any sort, no. Of all the tools in the shed, I would put up one, Mr. Haggard, as the dullest blade of all. When I looked into his eyes, I saw a fog that perpetually stayed in the harbor.

Coming up from the ranks of football coach, P.E. and Drivers Ed. combination, he was hired primarily as a disciplinarian. He was a hulk of a man and his presence in the hallway and at school events was a deterrent to misbehaving. However, he felt uncomfortable in this one-dimensional role and felt obligated to put some words of wisdom out there for the faculty and student body.

One place he liked to do this was to include in the daily announcements a segment called "Principles from the Principal." Mr. Haggard thought this title was the height of wittiness, even though most of each day's bulletin was about housekeeping matters that had nothing to do with lofty thoughts. But he liked to add his parting shot of wisdom with a quote that he had his secretary dig up from some book of quotes. For instance, "That which does not kill us makes us stronger." There was never an attribution to the quote, as if he had thought of this Nietzsche quote himself. Or "We are all born ignorant, but one must work hard to remain stupid"; again, not attributed (Benjamin Franklin) and not a quote that he saw any irony in.

One year I was appointed to look over the daily announcements ("Principles from the Principal" was included) for grammar and other language errors, and then to make sure that I selected an intelligent senior to read them over the PA. After a while, I found the quotes didn't do much for anyone except the principal. So, I decided to replace them with some of my own quotes. AND I would give attributions.

"And finally, for Mr. Haggard's 'Principles from Principal' quote of the day, 'A man with a wrench can release life-giving waters.' Christopher Plumber." That was my first day's work. Soon to be followed by:

"Education is the means by which we can soar and look down on others." Ima Prig

"The road of excess leads to the throne of porcelain." Upton Chuck

"The soul is to be found camping out in the brain's alley ways." Abdullah Oblongata

After a week of this, my fellow teachers in the faculty lounge said, "Settle, we know what you've been up to. And it's the first time that any of us have listened to the quote of the day. Some of our students have caught on, too. Do you mind if we make some contributions?"

And so it was, we had our fun for about a semester before Principal Haggard began to become suspicious of all the congratulations he received on the quotes. A few teachers carried this out even further by asking for the principal's elucidation on quotes like "Make iron your arm and your pen-hand molten" by Richard Steele or "There is no royal road to learning except in yellow jackets" by Clifford Notez. Haggard would look puzzled, and then ask them to repeat the quote. As I said previously, the fog never rose, so he would reply, "I don't remember putting that in the bulletin, but they sound like words to live by." Archimedes' principle states that the average **density** of an object is what ultimately determines whether it floats – Principal Haggard never floated.

And by a Sleep to Say

There are always those students who find the sounds of the classroom like white noise and succumb easily into arms of Morpheus, especially after lunch or on days when the thermostat is set a bit too high. One of these students was Jason Lasseur.

Jason was a very intelligent student, but he liked to read what he wanted to read. I often caught him with a book hidden inside the book he was supposed to be reading. He, also, liked his learning to be experiential, and he roamed the city at night meeting all sorts of people and writing notes to prepare for his goal of becoming a writer. Because of his interest in writing, I put up with quite a bit from him. But one day, I thought I'd give him some material for a story.

Jason had fallen into a deep sleep at the beginning of the period. And even if I called his name, he didn't budge with his head on his textbook, arms hanging to his sides like a leopard resting on a limb. Drool ran from the corner of his mouth onto the desktop. With five minutes left in class, I put my finger to my lips and pointed to Jason. Then I went to the clock and advanced it a few hours. The class packed up silently and tiptoed out of the class. I turned off the lights and softly closed the door.

The door had a large window and many kids remained staring at Lasseur to see when he would awaken. This was the period right before lunch hour, and it got pretty loud at the change of periods. The bell went off, and we could see Jason move slightly as he was coming to. An eye popped open. You could see he was trying to orient himself as to his location in time and space. After a few seconds, his head popped up like a jack-in-the-box – no one was in the class and the whole room was darkened. He looked at the clock and jerked out of his desk frantically. Both he and the desk tipped over and his books were strewn onto the floor. Later, we found out that his legs had fallen asleep and he could not stand.

He crawled desperately along the floor trying to gather his books and get up. At that moment, the door flew open and lights came on full blast. Jason Lasseur squinted like a cave creature suddenly exposed to light. He covered his eyes with his arm and was helped to his feet by a group of classmates, who were laughing so hard they were panting.

"Is school over? What time is it?" They led him out of the classroom to the cafeteria. Jason became the story of the day and a story that remained years to come. Jason Lasseur continued to surreptitiously read other materials in my class, but he never fell asleep again. 'Twas a consummation that I devoutly wished.

The Proud Student's Contumely

In the same vein of punishment to fit the crime, I had Jeanne Koepp. She was a top student and involved in many aspects of the school. She was constantly late for class because of one meeting or another – yearbook, fundraising projects, school government, etc. I was very understanding about her tardiness, because of her contributions to the school and because she always made sure that she kept up with whatever was assigned at the beginning of class.

Unfortunately for her, one of the teachers informed me that she saw Jeanne on a number of occasions slowly making her way to class, reading bulletin boards and poking her head into the library to talk to someone. When Mrs. Stollen questioned her about where she belonged, she told the librarian that Mr. Settle didn't care if she was late for class. "Oh-ho," I thought. "your privilege has turned into disrespect. Perhaps, it's lesson plan time for you."

On a day that Ms. Koepp was leisurely making her way back to senior English, I quickly instructed the class on what to do when she appeared. No one seemed to have any problems with pranking Ms. Perfect, Jeanne, and some took to it with a relish.

When Jeanne came through the door and was taking her seat, I said, "Okay, all of you put your books away, and we'll have a test on Chapter 7." Koepp looked stunned. You could see her looking around in disbelief. She whispered to those around her, who assured her that the test had been announced yesterday. Everyone kept strict control over any smiles and waited for me to verbally give them each question.

"Question number one. In 500 words or more, why was Lord Ashton in the essay 'The Merits of Slavery' resigned to the fact that Africans were an inferior race?" Pencils flew across the papers. There seemed to be quite a bit to say about this topic. Jeanne, not to be easily defeated, joined the graphite fest, adding her 500 words to the question.

After everyone seemed to be done on question one, I moved to question two. "Which did you find more insightful – the short piece 'Corpse Digger' or 'Living with Roosters' and why? (A few here had to cough in order to keep control.) Just 200 words here." Again, pencils took off like a burst of pigeons. And again, Jeanette remained valiant in her efforts to put down something.

"And the last question. Who is the student in class that is not in on the charade of a test? You may shout out this answer."

"JEANNE KOEPP!"

Amidst the taking off the masks and hubbub, I took her written responses off her desk and read them to the class. It was a masterful example of taking what little context was available and writing gobbledygook. The entire class was in admiration of her fortitude in not going down without a fight.

Afterwards, I did talk to Jeanne about what constitutes acceptable tardiness. I, also, told her what had been observed in her lack of alacrity in returning to my class and what she had said about my lackadaisical attitude toward her being late. The issue was resolved without any punishment. Further, Jeanne Koepp was a person with a great sense of humor, and she rather enjoyed the notoriety of being fooled. Of course, knowing Jeanne's fortitude, I wondered whether I was in for some prank in the future.

Redrum Most Foul

What would a chapter on pranks be without a haunted house episode? Sometimes a prank falls right into one's lap. In this case, I was involved with a senior class that was the most superstitious group that I'd ever encountered. Two of my students, who were vying for valedictorian of their class, dropped out of the senior play when they found out that it had a séance in it. No matter that the séance was in the context of a comedy and performed by a shyster channeler (something like Whoopi Goldberg in *Ghost*). No, anything having to do with devils, witches, Ouija boards, ghosts was *verboten* to their religious beliefs.

As much as I respected their beliefs, I told the class that I didn't believe in "no" ghosts. That's when I learned about THE HOUSE. Who knew how old THE HOUSE was or how long it had decayed on the side of a mountain, but all agreed it was evil. There were many stories of murders that had occurred there – one that went as far back as the murder of a Cherokee shaman, who continued to roam the area.

"I'd like to go there myself to check it out," I said.

"For God's sake, no, Mr. Settle! We're not kidding. That house is eee-vil. Don't do it."

"Who'd be willing to take me? I want to go at night to give the ghosts a fair chance," I said cavalierly.

No one seemed to think that was funny. But I did manage to get a few reluctant volunteers, mostly young men that were afraid but brave. With less than enthusiastic cooperation, we arranged a time and a meeting place. More people could come if they wanted.

When I arrived at the assigned place at the base of the mountain, there were many more people waiting than I had anticipated. Word had gotten around the school, and there were more students that wanted to stick a toe into the spirit world. I had a small backpack with me and a large, six-volt flashlight. It was fall and a bit chilly. "Well, let's go meet the Medicine Man. Where's the path?" Their laughter was a bit thin.

Everyone turned on their (yes, I'm aware "everyone" is singular) flashlights. I was glad a few seniors were familiar with the trail because it was covered with leaves and difficult to see. Our steps in the leaves became amplified in everyone's silence. Suddenly we stopped. The student in the lead pointed to a tree. He whispered, "Someone was tied to this tree and riddled with bullets. See the bullet holes." I looked more closely and, indeed, the tree was riddled with holes, but from past experience, I identified these as woodpecker feeding holes. But I nodded solemnly and put my fingers into a few of the holes.

As we continued, a number of students were having second thoughts about challenging any evil spirits. They decided that they were going no farther than the execution tree. They would wait for our return. As our ranks thinned, I could tell that those who remained were getting a bit jumpy as they started at any little sound from breeze to sticks snapping to owls hooting. It wasn't a pitch-black night, and the moon was full enough to make out some of our surroundings even without flashlights. Soon I could make out a gray mass up ahead that was the dilapidated cabin. A profound hush came over our band of exorcists. We began using hand signals. I made a circle with a finger, and all of us slowly made our way around the abandoned shack.

The porch roof had collapsed and fallen over the door, but I did see a side entrance through a window. I pointed at the window and then made little walking movements with my fingers. I noticed as I approached the window, no one followed (just as I had hoped). I put one foot over the windowsill and then ducked to bring the rest of my body through. I combed the area with my flashlight – an old woodstove in disrepair, a floor shot through with crumbling boards, a few rusted porcelain pots, and some beer and whisky bottles (apparently the spirits liked spirits). Then I shuffled off my backpack and took out my hidden boom box. I put in the tape that I had made the day before: selections from *The Exorcist* soundtrack and *Songs of the Humpback Whale*. I placed the box close to the window and started off with a low volume that I gradually increased. Suddenly I switched my light off and yelled, "Oh, god, no." The music went up to full blast as I put a shaky leg out the window that was quickly pulled back in.

When I looked out the window, everyone was on the move. I shined my light down the pathway, and some were leaping down the mountainside like fleeing mountain goats. I gathered up my stuff and began to make my way back to our assignation point. The pathway was sufficiently beaten down to make the trip back easy.

I was flooded with questions: "What happened up there? How'd you get away? Are you okay? What got ahold of you?" I opened my backpack and took out my recorder and played them a few segments of the music.

It was a night they'd never forget. And later, students described with relish the unknown running abilities of fellow classmates. Some suggested that they should go out for track in the spring. While I hadn't changed anybody's minds about the spirit world, I did manage to put across a healthy skepticism about such things. THE HAUNTED HOUSE became just a haunted house after that – a place to take others to scare the wits out of them. And at school reunions, there are those that talk about that night and the almost weightless scamper down a mountainside.

Water Gun Discipline

Did students prank me? You betcha. I liked to create an atmosphere in class where there was tacit approval to have some fun at my expense. Mostly, I was the recipient of dropping pencils at a prescribed time, chalk in the eraser, and making odd sounds when my back was turned. However, there were some creative efforts where I was justly humbled.

Occasionally during the school year, I would shake up my usual methods of discipline with what I called "water gun discipline." If a student wasn't paying attention, passing a note, cheating, or sleeping, he or she got squirted. It's an embarrassment to catch a stream of water in the face when you're not expecting it. Water gun discipline was effective but obnoxious.

Usually, I put the water gun away before I became too annoying. But there was one year where water-gun power went to my head, and I became too trigger-happy. A couple of students I'd spray for wrong answers or asking too many questions or forgetting their homework. As you might expect, one class had had enough.

Teachers can sense when something is afoot. When I walked into class, I could see the students were all settled in their desks and smiling at me with bonhomie. If you are a male teacher, you quickly drift behind the podium (Isn't that why we have podiums?) and check your zipper. I was zipped up – so that wasn't it. Cautiously after the bell, I began class, taking out my water gun and placing it on the desk so that I could write on the board.

When I turned around, the entire class was standing. They had every kind of water gun known to man (a few were pump-action the size of a sawed-off shotgun), and they were locked and loaded. I made a quick move for my pistol, but I was showered with water in the way Bonnie and Clyde were machine-gunned in the movie. I managed a few meek returns of fire. But they soaked me to the bone before I could escape out the side door.

A few of my turncoat colleagues were waiting for me outside the door. They had aided and abetted the class's effort to get me. They led me back into the classroom like Nathan Hale to the delight of all – yes, even me. It was truly an outrageous and legendary coup. My water gun was confiscated, only to be collected at the end of the school year. Was I dissuaded from ever using water-gun discipline again? Of course not. But I was more attuned to its excesses and the dangers of revenge.

"Take the Bite Out of Crime"

There are "gifted" students that are able with an uncanny accuracy to label the faculty or administrators with a nickname. These nicknames are – what can I say – usually *perfect*. One teacher was called "Hopper," and, indeed, he looked and moved like a grasshopper. Another was "Duck," whose nose and chin almost met like a duckbill. My nom de plume was "Brillo," as I had hair like a wirehaired terrier.

The vice principal at one school I taught at was called "McGruff." It wasn't so much that VP Thomas Radcliffe looked like the bloodhound cartoon character of "Take a Bite Out of Crime"; it was his "snoop" disposition. "McGruff" was in charge of school discipline, and he roamed the recesses of school, a Barney Fife looking for any small infraction to enforce.

His greatest obsession was quelling the pot-smoking epidemic. And, indeed, we did have our pot smokers, who I immediately recognized by the glowing film on their eyes. I would always take them aside and tell them if they ever came again to my class high, there would be consequences. That was usually enough, considering the usual paranoia that went with smoking weed. But Radcliffe went after these kids with the zeal of an officer of the Inquisition. He was constantly sleuthing the hallways, lockers, and small niches sniffing for any evidence of marijuana. He longed to be the righteous god that came down on this abomination with the fury of Yahweh of the Torah.

I remember once as I was walking down the hallway, he hailed me.

"Mr. Settle, I would like you to come into the boys' bathroom and smell."

I responded with Bartleby the Scrivener's famous epithet, "I prefer not to."

But he dragged me into the restroom where I could smell among other things the pungent aroma of pot.

"You were a hippie, Settle. You know all about drugs. Is that MARIJUANA?"

"Well, of course, I haven't partaken in quite a while, and there are some competing odors to sort through. But

I do believe I can smell pot – not the toilet bowls, sir – weed."

"AH-HA! They're not going to get away with it in MY school!"

His face twitched like a small terrier on a leash ready to take on a German shepherd. He thought he was up to the task, but I knew this evidence was going to lead him into a small corner of hell.

Once it was apparent that McGruff was on a new campaign to end the use of weed in the school (and the world at large), the pranks began. Students started leaving fake joints in selected places all over the school. Even students who had never smoked pot began learning to roll joints filled with oregano so they could participate in the torture. Crumpled notes filled with vague details of drug buys and meeting places began to litter the hallways, toilets, and parking lots. Radcliffe was being constantly tapped on the shoulder only to turn and find no one there.

He brought in the film *Reefer Madness* – that classically excessive and unintentionally funny exposé of the dangers of marijuana. When the students were rolling in the aisles at the antics of the sallow-face reefer addicts, VP flicked on the lights in moral outrage. He proceeded to give them an indignant, red-faced sermon along the lines of Jonathan Edwards's "Sinners in the Hands of an Angry God."

McGruff was sleuthing himself into a phosphorescent pit. Mary Jane was glowing in the dark everywhere, yet he was unable to reach out and catch a perpetrator. He began looking like one of the gaunt addicts in the reefer movie. I could take it no longer nor could a few of the merry pranksters that I talked to. They realized they had gone too far and that it was time to stop.

Suddenly, the endless supply of joints, faux notes, and incense smells ceased – POOF! McGruff was puzzled at first but having the kind of opaque ego that he did, he accredited his efforts as the cause. "They knew I was closing in, Mr. Settle. I think we safely weathered this crisis, at least for a while, don't you think?"

"Yes, Mc...Mr. Radcliffe, I think you were able to rise to the occasion. Your efforts were truly risible, and you've served the needs of the students. Well done. Well done."

Conclusion: The Prank that Kept on Giving

Each class has its own personality. For teachers, how students are going to interact as a group is very much like what Forrest Gump's mother had to say, "Life is like a box of chocolates. You never know what you're gonna get." After a few days with a particular freshman English class, I felt that I had lucked out. What I was going to get was a group that was inquisitive, smart, and funny.

After a few weeks with this class, I found it easy, almost too easy, to digress. For some reason that I can't remember, we digressed to the subject of Donny and Marie Osmond. The brother and sister duo had a successful variety show at the time, and I told the class that they repulsed me.

Well, that started a furor. How could anybody not like the sweetness, beauty, and purity of Donny and Marie. In a humorous vain, I told them that diabetes ran in my family and that I was afraid that being exposed to all that sweetness would make it kick in. In a more serious fashion, I said that they put forth an image that was too perfect. I liked my entertainers to be a bit more in touch with the gritty side of life. Donny and Marie were nothing more than hair and teeth commercials. The digression ended quickly, and I thought no more about it.

When I met with this class the next day, I had a number of things to write on the board. As I was writing, I began to hear music, but I couldn't make it out. When I turned to the class, I heard nothing at all. I chalked it up (no pun intended) to some melody coming through the window from the music department. Then, it happened again, although this time the music was louder. When I looked out over the class, everyone was deadpan. The music then streamed out in high volume, and I located it under the desk of a freckled-face, red-haired freshman. The class burst into laughter. The melody was "A Little Bit Country, A Little Bit Rock 'N Roll" by none other than Donny and Marie Osmond.

It's rare that freshmen feel comfortable enough to prank the teacher. I took it as a compliment and laughed at their audacity. Two students were responsible for this caper – Aaron Dubik and Tracy Chancellor. Aaron, the red-haired boy, was the picture of Tom Sawyer, if you wanted to cast a movie. Tracy was a shy and soft-spoken wit with a twinkle in her eyes. After this event, I took notice of them in a way I never would have done had they not played this trick on me.

In fact, thirty-five years later, we are dear friends (not teacher-student friends). They have watched me grow old, and I have watched them grow up. They've been with me through marriage, divorce, triumphs, and tragedies as I have been with them through their relationships and middle-age crises. At one time, Tracy's baby and my baby played together in my living room. And it all started with a prank, a prank that has never stopped giving.

Chapter 8

Wasting Time Efficiently:
Three Lessons on Poetry

I fear that the trade-off for efficiency in education is a lack of depth. "Wasting time" in American culture is equivalent to what mortal sin was in Catholicism – it's the pathway to Hell. In order not to dawdle, our culture offers us many ways to save time and to get down to the essence so that we can quickly move on toward our goals.

Evelyn Wood would provide me with my first challenge to this philosophy of focused efficiency. Ms. Wood developed a system of speed reading that was very influential in the 1960s when I was in college. How wonderful it sounded to spend half the time (or less) doing all the reading that I needed to do for my classes (especially being an English major). Therefore, I enrolled in one of her classes with the romance of launching into the river of knowledge with a speedboat rather than a rowboat.

I read down the middle of the page with my finger as a pointer; I read words in groups or phrases; I didn't reread; and I didn't subvocalize. After a month of trying to read this way, I found I hated it. I loved to dawdle over words, I loved to masticate good prose, I loved to reread passages in order to understand them better. If anything, I was less capable of engaging a text using the Wood method. I could identify with the underlying truth of Woody Allen's quote, "I took a speed reading course where you run your finger down the middle of the page and was able to read *War and Peace* in twenty minutes. It's about Russia."

Thus, in the Jurassic, I never worried too much about a sub-corollary of wasting time, "covering material." If you have to "cover material," you often smother material. It becomes a kind of Jeopardy game of knowing the definition of a sonnet without encountering the beauty of sonnets.

In this chapter, I will go over three of my lesson plans to teach poetry. They definitely are not efficient, and they definitely waste time. The questions are – are they a waste of time? does effective trump efficient? did I choose the pathway to Hell like Huckleberry Finn?

One Hen, Two Ducks

I am a great believer in the value of students memorizing poems, soliloquies, great speeches, and quotes. Once passages get into long-term memory, people can keep an author's eloquence like a tattoo for the rest of their lives. The phrase I like better than *memorizing* is "learning by heart," because this is a way for literature to get into the heart, even though it may take years to make its way. All of my classes during a semester had a memorization assignment. And before I revealed that assignment, I always introduced it with the following exercise:

The bell would ring for the start of the period, and I would stand at the head of the first row of desks and without any explanation, I would ask the first person to repeat after me, "one hen." Then I moved to the next student and asked him to repeat, "one hen, two ducks." Then onto the next, "one hen, two ducks, three squawking geese." When I got to the fourth item in the sequence, I could feel a growing concentration as the students began to realize the rules of the game..."four Limerick oysters."

The list was getting longer and those whom I was moving toward began fidgeting in their seats – "one hen, two ducks, three squawking geese, four Limerick oysters, five corpulent porpoises." (A tittering from the class as someone had to repeat all of these.) "...six pairs of Don Alverzo's tweezers." The tension was building, the class was focused, and the laughter more pronounced. "...seven thousand Macedonians dressed in full battle array" and then "...eight shiny brass monkeys from the ancient sacred crypts of Egypt." As the list became longer, I had students that were unable to repeat it. If that were the case, I would move to the next student and not add on another item to remember. I kept doing this until someone remembered them all, and then I would increase the list for the next student. I usually stopped at eight and then went around the room until everybody could recite the eight.

So, what would be the point of doing this exercise? The exercise showed everyone that memorizing wasn't that hard; it takes no particular intellectual skills, just dogged repetition until you get the words into your long-term memory. I would tell the class that if you can remember the nonsensical list that I had just given you, you should have no trouble with Robert Frost's "The Road Not Taken."

I could have written on the chalkboard homework area, "Memorize Robert Frost's 'The Road Not Taken' by Monday, October 4. You will recite it or write it out," and have done away with this small drama. In this way, I could have parceled out more time to *cover more material*. But for me, that would have been deadly dull and not as encouraging to students to accomplish the assignment. Instead, I chose the road less traveled by and that made all the difference.

For those interested in the entire list, which was created in the early days of radio to test announcers, here it is:

- One hen
- Two ducks
- Three squawking geese
- Four Limerick oysters
- Five corpulent porpoises
- Six pairs of Don Alverzo's tweezers
- Seven thousand Macedonians dressed in full battle array
- Eight shiny brass monkeys from the ancient sacred crypts of Egypt
- Nine apathetic, sympathetic, diabetic old men on roller skates, with a marked propensity towards procrastination and sloth
- Ten lyrical, spherical, diabolical denizens of the deep who all stall around the corner of the quo of the quay of the quivery, all at the same time

To Parody or Not to Parody

Most of us like to parody. It's entertaining. It's fun. When I was growing up, I loved to get the most recent issue of *Mad Magazine* to see what they had done to popular song lyrics and, certainly, Weird Al Yankovic made a living out of parodying pop music. But other than entertainment, what can a teacher do with parody in the classroom?

In my case, I liked to use a few of Weird Al's songs in order to introduce parody, and I liked to sound out students about any parodies they knew about (they all knew a few, and they always were good for some laughs). I, also, liked to share a few that I'd written myself. But then I moved onto some poem or passage of literature that I wanted them to parody.

More than most things, English teachers want to teach their students to read closely. Literature can't be skimmed like the newspaper. Parody unconsciously forces a close reading. If you're going to rewrite the lines of a poem, you have to look closely at those lines. It often happens that as students begin parodying a poem, they become more familiar with the words and lines of the poem itself and concomitantly begin to understand it more.

Let's take Shakespeare, as an example. "Bill" is difficult for most students, especially with the strange rhythms, vocabularies, and annotations. Getting students to concentrate on and stick with Shakespeare requires vitamin pills and immunization shots. That's why I had them do a parody of the famous "To be or not to be" soliloquy.

First, let's look at the original:

Hamlet's "To Be or Not To Be" Soliloquy[1]

To be, or not to be[2] – that is the question: 1
Whether 'tis nobler in the mind to suffer
The slings and arrows of outrageous fortune
Or to take arms against a sea of troubles
And by opposing end them.[3] To die, to sleep[4] –   5
No more – and by a sleep to say we end
The heartache, and the thousand natural shocks
That flesh is heir to. 'Tis a consummation
Devoutly to be wished.[5] To die, to sleep –
To sleep – perchance to dream: ay, there's the rub,   10
For in that sleep of death what dreams may come
When we have shuffled off this mortal coil,[6]
Must give us pause. There's the respect
That makes calamity of so long life.[7]
For who would bear the whips and scorns of time,   15
Th' oppressor's wrong, the proud man's contumely,[8]
The pangs of despised love, the law's delay,
The insolence of office, and the spurns
That patient merit of th' unworthy takes,[9]
When he himself might his quietus[10] make   20
With a bare bodkin[11]?[12] Who would fardels[13] bear,
To grunt and sweat under a weary life,
But that the dread of something after death,[14]
The undiscovered country, from whose bourn
No traveller returns, puzzles the will,   25
And makes us rather bear those ills we have
Than fly to others that we know not of?[15]
Thus conscience does make cowards of us all,[16]
And thus the native hue of resolution
Is sicklied o'er with the pale cast of thought,[17]   30
And enterprises of great pitch and moment

With this regard their currents turn awry
And lose the name of action.[18] *– Soft you now,*
The fair Ophelia![19] *– Nymph, in thy orisons*
Be all my sins remembered.[20] *35*

Annotations

1. A solo speech given by an actor on stage.
2. "To be or not to be" means to live or to commit suicide.
3. Lines 3-5 "Whether 'tis" to "end them" – if we decide to live, we can take two approaches – suffer with dignity or fight the causes of our suffering and put an end to them.
4. "To die, to sleep" – however, we can decide to die, which can be a kind of sleep.
5. Lines 6-9 "by a sleep" to "devoutly to be wished" – sleep sounds pretty good.
6. Lines 10-12 "to sleep" to "mortal coil" – sleeping might not be so good because the sleep of death may include dreams. "Mortal coil" is one's body.
7. Lines 13-14 say that we should take a moment to reflect on what it means to live a long life.
8. "Contumely" is an insolent or arrogant remark or act.
9. Lines 15-19 are a list of all the reasons that it's not advantageous to live a long life.
10. "Quietus" means a release from life.
11. "Bare bodkin" is the naked blade of a stilleto.
12. Lines 19-20 finish the initial question by saying isn't it better to kill oneself with a knife that put up with all suffering of a long life.
13. "Fardels" are bundled burdens.

14. Line 23 – the fear of what is going to happen to us after we die.
15. Lines 24-27 – the idea of an afterlife makes us bear life's suffering rather than trying other solutions.
16. Line 28 – our conscience keeps us from killing ourselves for fear of going to Hell.
17. Lines 29-30 – our thoughts about going to Hell undermine our resolve to commit suicide.
18. Lines 31-33 – we are unable to do great things because our consciences get in the way and keep us from acting.
19. Lines 33-34 – Hamlet tells himself to be quiet because he sees Ophelia enter the stage.
20. Lines 34-35 – *Orisons* are prayers, and Hamlet hopes that beautiful Ophelia asks in her prayers that Hamlet be forgiven for his sins.

Who would **fardels** bear? My spell check can't bear them. My students can't bear them. Is **orisons** pronounced like horizons? Do you find **bare bodkins** at nudist colonies? And is **quietus** nap time? When doing parody, students are forced into all sorts of detail from meanings, pronunciations, etymologies, and contexts. Next, I showed them a parody of this speech that I had written:

Soliloquy of a Couch Potato
Tuber or not tuber, that is the question:
Whether 'tis nobler in the mind to suffer
The slings and eros of Wheel of Fortune,
Or to take arms against a sea of products,
And by opposing end them. To diet, to eat –
No more – and by what we eat to say we end

The heart attack and the thousand natural shocks
That flesh is heir to. 'Tis a consummation
Devoutly to be wished. To diet, to eat;
To eat, a potato with sour cream; Ay, there's the rub,
For in that spud of death what dreams may come
When we have shuffled off this mortal foil,
Must give us pause. There's the respect
That makes calamity of so long life.
For who would bear the whips and scorns of eating out,
The oppressive prong, the overpriced consommé,
The pangs of hunger, the slaw's delay,
The insolence of waiters, and the spurns
That patient merit of th' unworthy takes
When he himself might his quiet time take
With a bare sofa? Who would fart in chairs
To grunt and sweat under a weary life,
But that the hope of something after work,
The undiscovered cable from whose bourn
No traveler returns, nuzzles the will
And makes us rather bear those ills we have
Than fly to others that we know not of?
Thus television makes cowards of us all;
And thus the native hue of resolution
Is sicklied o'er with the pale cast of sitcoms,
And enterprises of great pitch and moment
With this remote their currents turn awry;
And lose the name of action. – Soft you now,
The fair Oprah. Nymph, in thy orisons
Be all my sins remembered.

Looking at both the original and the parody becomes a
humorous kind of comparative literature. I don't ask my

students for a parody that is as complete as mine, but I do ask that they start off with a theme using Hamlet's first line, the most famous line in all of Shakespeare – to punt or not to punt, to cheat or not to cheat, Tudor or not Tudor, two-door or not two-door – and try to carry it out till the end. This is a group assignment, and there can be a lot of fun for all. More importantly, they will be more familiar with that soliloquy than they ever would with just a recitation of it.

I can see that some would say this assignment is a mutilation of Shakespeare and a waste of time while we could be covering more of the play. And I would respond that the very sacredness of Shakespeare requires some iconoclasm. There is too much praise of Shakespeare, making him an elitist pleasure. At first, I think students find it hard to believe that commoners vied for spots in the Globe Theater. Further, that "Bill" was bawdy and appealed to lower sensibilities. Parody makes Bill an author like other authors and not a demi-god.

A couple other well-known pieces that I liked to use for parodying exercises (and quite a bit easier than the lengthy Hamlet soliloquy) were Robert Frost's "Fire and Ice" and the famous prayer the "Our Father."

Fire and Ice
Some say the world will end in fire,
Some say in ice.
From what I've tasted of desire
I hold with those who favor fire.
But if it had to perish twice,
I think I know enough of hate
To say that for destruction ice

Is also great
And would suffice.

In an age of technological hubris, this parody was a good way to think about the many ways the world could end. It was an awareness-building exercise that taught science, politics, and the rhythms of a famous poem. At the time, "gray goo" of nanotechnology was one way it could end and so was bioterrorism. Thus, we have:

Addendum to "Fire and Ice"
Some say the world will end in bioterror,
Some say in nanotech,
From what I've tasted of computer error,
I hold with those who favor terror.
But if it twice should go to heck,
I think I know enough about gray goo
To say that for destruction nanotech
Would also do
To nice effect.

Perhaps the easiest parody that I used was the "Our Father," which many people already knew by heart. The parody had to do with taking a scientific concept that was rather new and putting it into prayer, thus making it more accessible and humorous to the non-scientist. Sometimes I had a science teacher come in and talk about cutting-edge concepts in science and technology and the vocabulary that went with them. Some examples:

The Our Ozone

Our O$_3$,
which art in heaven,
halogens flee thy name.
Thy kingdom come
without carbon
on earth
as it is in heaven.
Give us this day
our daily rays
and free us of bad air conditions
as we freon our air conditioners.
And lead us not
into radiation
but deliver us from UV,
for thine is the fusion,
the absorption,
and the layer
for every
human.

A second example:

Clone Father

Clone Father,
whose art is heaven,
hallowed be guanine.
Thy sequence come
a new genome
at birth as it is in vitro.
Give us DNA, our GM bread,
and forgive us our transgenics

as transgenics replaces those against us.
And Linnaeus not into classification
but deliver us from species.
For thymine is the Kingdom,
and the Phylum and Gregory,
forever,
J. Mendel.

Scanning in the Jurassic

In the Jurassic, when you scanned a poem, you didn't put it into digital form. You looked for those pesky anapests, little lamb iambs, pensive pentameters and curséd hexameters. You counted accented and unaccented syllables. And you always knew that Shakespeare wrote blank verse in iambic pentameter, even though you had little idea of what that meant.

My lesson plan for teaching the scanning of poetry was writing limericks. "Surely you jest, Mr. Settle" some of you might say since:

A limerick packs laughs anatomical
Into space that is quite economical.
But the good ones I've seen
So seldom are clean
And the clean ones so seldom comical.

Contrary to the above limerick, I did want to be comical while at the same time keeping it clean. In my early years, I tried to teach stylized verse by having my classes write sonnets, but the form was too long, advanced, and stodgy to get a real sense of count and emphasis. On the other hand, the limerick was short, and it could easily be pointed out when the rhythm went wrong. And finally, most of the class was already familiar with the limerick (yes, the salacious ones), even though they didn't exactly know how they worked as a poetic form.

They worked only if they kept a strict adherence to this formula:

- five lines with a rhyme scheme of a-a-b-b-a
- lines 1, 2, and 5 must have three feet each
- lines 3 and 4 must contain two feet
- the feet of the limerick are mostly anapests (dih-dih-Dah) and iambs (dih-Dah) and an occasional unaccented syllable

Thus, a limerick would rhythmically be like this:
dih-Dah dih-dih-Dah dih-dih-Dah-dih
dih-dih-Dah dih-dih-Dah dih-dih-Dah-dih
dih-Dah dih-dih-Dah
dih-dih-Dah dih-dih-Dah
dih-dih-Dah dih-dih-Dah dih-dih-Dah-dih

I usually selected a few themes they could pursue. They could write a limerick about me, the principal, vice principal, or a politician. They could write limericks about authors and characters in books. They could **not** write limericks about each other or other teachers. They, also, had to use the accent marks above their limerick's syllables. This is typical of what I got:

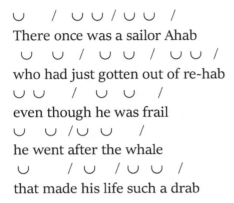

∪　　／　∪ ∪ ／ ∪ ∪　／
There once was a sailor Ahab
　∪　　∪　／　∪　∪　／　∪ ∪　／
who had just gotten out of re-hab
∪ ∪　　／　∪　∪　／
even though he was frail
∪　　∪ ／∪　∪　　／
he went after the whale
　∪　　　／ ∪　／ ∪ ∪　／
that made his life such a drab

Certainly, not something that will be preserved for future generations, but accessible, informative, and witty.

Internalize that rhythm and you'll soon be identifying feet, meters, and rhyme schemes, which can be applied to more complex stylized forms like sonnets, blank verse, and villanelles. Not only will you be able to identify these poetic terms, you'll also be capable of writing them and appreciating those that have mastered them.

But that's my "Steady as she goes" philosophy, which doesn't teach to a test and doesn't worry about covering material.

I leave you, dear reader, with one of my favorite limericks, written by that ubiquitous poet of all ages: A. Nonymous:

There once was a beautiful lass
Who went to a beach, Boston, Mass.
She stepped in the bay
On one balmy day.
The water was up to her knees.

(This limerick rhymes when the tide comes in.)
Sorry. Iamb irrepressible; anapest.

Conclusion:

In the 80s, I wrote an editorial piece for *The Decatur Herald and Review*, the newspaper in Decatur, IL. It was in opposition to a previous article about class size. The author was one of those efficiency people who claimed research and statistics proved that the differences between class sizes of 20 and 40 were insignificant. Therefore, we should begin making classes larger and save ourselves some money with teacher salaries.

I include this article at the end of this chapter because it reinforces its theme: efficiency and covering material often leaves out many variables in the educational process – some of them intangible. In the Jurassic, I was given time and freedom to pursue lesson plans that would probably be questionable today.

Statistics don't measure classroom quality

I don't think anything about human values can be proven with statistics. Statistics can point the way, support a conclusion, but they can never, in the final analysis, prove anything about issues that run deep in the human psyche.

Why? Because problems of great complexity just have too many variables and because many problems about human nature have too many intangibles.

Concerning Dale Eckhard's letter to the editor Feb. 21, I must say that I wholeheartedly disagree with his statistically based conclusions. Mr. Eckhard contends that research supports the notion that bigger class sizes will not seriously affect the quality of classroom instruction. According to him, research shows pupil-teacher ratios from 20:1 to 40:1 reveal "no significant effect on educational results as measured by student performances."

As a high school teacher, I find the glibness of the previous quote quite chilling. Chilling because there are going to be people who will believe the simplicity of that statement – indignant people with a splinter of truth who are going to support movements to cut back on teaching staffs in the schools.

I've seen studies like those Mr. Eckhard refers to. They are far from conclusive. Often, they are done with specialized groups (college-bound students) and specialized schools (not inner-city schools). Furthermore, they are often done over short periods of time and in classes that suit measurement like mathematics.

But these objections aside, I still do not believe that any study based on statistical analysis can ever include all the complex variables that go into learning. I rest this part of my argument on the illusive and elusive attempts of this century to measure human intelligence.

Secondly, there are many intangibles that cannot be measured when a group goes from 20 to 40 students. I take research very seriously when it makes some sense, but when someone tells me that the qualitative atmosphere of a classroom is the same whether I'm teaching 20 or 40 students, all I can say is that this doesn't match up to my experience or to any other teacher's experience that I have talked with. The sociology of a class changes radically from 20 to 40, as radically as when the temperature goes from 40 to 20. The result in both cases is ice.

Teachers dealing with 40 students are forced into certain rigid structures. Because of the increased paper load, they start giving more objective tests rather than essay tests. The discipline in class becomes more of a problem not only because of more physical bodies but because of the inability of a teacher to form attachments that allow discipline to flow from his/her personality. And lastly, the distance between learner and teacher becomes greater because the teacher is forced into the lecture mode to keep control of the class.

This relationship between student and mentor, I believe, is one of those intangibles that is overlooked in many people's analysis of the learning process. Yet, I am firmly convinced that the best learning I've ever done was done because of good, happy, friendly relationships I have had with teachers – relationships that just can't survive in crowded classrooms.

In conclusion, I can only say that I have a daughter who will be starting school in a few years. If I am given the choice between sending her to a school where the pupil-teacher ratio is 20:1 or to a school where the ratio is 40:1, you can be assured that I will not listen to Mr. Eckhard's cited research. I will be concerned with care and nurturance. Does anyone know the statistics for those words?

Chapter 9

The Great Awk

One of the handiest (and ineffective) proofreading marks for English teachers during the Jurassic was *awk*. *Awk* stood for *awkward* and blanketed a host of unspecific writing problems. It was supposed to be used to signal the student that he or she needed to rephrase an *awkward* sentence or paragraph. However, it was mostly used when you either had no idea how to fix a student's bad writing or you could not read their cursive but felt obliged to make some sort of comment. So, you'd write "awk sent" or "awk," using the pilcrow to symbolize paragraph.

Thankfully, the greatness of *awk* as a proofreading term went the way of extinction as did the bird, the great auk. I'm appropriating it here to refer to those moments in my teaching career that I have witnessed or experienced some high-powered awkwardness, embarrassment, or disgrace. These stories range from the sublime to the ridiculous and the profound to the pitiful. Many I continue to recall with a wince no matter where I am or what I'm doing. Others raise me up and encourage me to never stop [si*] facing my fears.

*split infinitive. Another proofreading abbreviation that has rightly gone the way of extinction.

Wretch in the Works

I had trepidations as class sponsor about going on the senior class trip. It wasn't the chaperoning that was bothering me – these kids were rock solid – but it was the destination, a ski resort in Minnesota. What I was afraid of was that I would almost surely succumb to pressures from everyone to ski, and I hadn't skied a day in my life. The vision that kept returning to my unguarded moments was a hospital room with an elevated plastered leg. I could hear the nurses whispering, "The doctor said he's never seen such a bad break. He'll walk again, but only with a severe limp." (Oh Lord, let this cup pass from me.)

I prayed that the ski resort would not have enough snow; that they'd be closed down for back taxes; that they'd have an outbreak of Legionnaires' disease. But all for naught. The day arrived for us to embark, and the report from the slopes was that the skiing conditions were excellent. "Okay, calm yourself, Settle. Just do the mature thing and deny this is happening."

Denial was easy. As is true for all senior trips, spirits were high: singing, joking, teasing, laughing, and screaming. The bus driver obviously had done this before, driving with a smile on his face protected by his high-dollar earplugs. I joined in on the folderol and took care to make sure everyone was included in the good time. As we headed north, the snow accumulations became more pronounced. "What, me worry?" Responsibility can be a way of running away from fear.

We arrived at the resort in the evening, and the seniors ran around the resort-like dogs released from a kennel. I sat in front of a roaring fire with a snifter of brandy contemplating my fate and building up my courage for the next morning's ski lessons. After bed check and a distribution of night watch assignments among parents on the trip, I fell into bed and into a troubled sleep with visions of three-pronged canes dancing in my head.

Snowplow – that was the salient point for me after our early morning ski lesson. No zigzagging for me. Just enjoy the gentle gravity on the bunny slope with ski tips pointed together and cruise to the bottom and waddle back to the top to do it again. I kept doing this until I realized that I was the only adult on this slightly graded hill. All the others had gone on to higher challenges; even Mamie Schuller, who had a leg damaged by polio, had moved on.

I looked to the right and there was the pathway back to the resort; I looked to the left and there was the pathway to the more difficult slopes. And both that morning equally lay, in snow that was trodden black. I chose the road less traveled by and ended up on a slope that had a revolving rope lift. You just held onto the rope like you were water skiing and the rope took you to the top. Easy-peasy.

I slipped and slid my way to the rope and fell down just at the point I was about to grab on the rope. In my frustration, I regained a standing position but not without making a serious blunder. My ski poles were wrapped around my wrist and, when I righted myself, they went onto the other side of the rope. As I cruised to the top, I had no idea this would be a problem until I let go of the rope and was not released.

The rope kept going and I kept going. Soon I was airborne, hanging by one arm with the ski pole straps folded over the rope. I looked up, and I was heading into the tower of the machine that encased a giant pulley. This would be my last sight before I was consumed in its gears. Frantically, I tried to wriggle myself off of the ropes. No good. And then I screamed with a fervor that I'm sure awakened the hibernating creatures of the forest. I closed my eyes as I approached the jaws that would either maim me or end my life.

I was about ten feet off the ground when everything stopped. It seems I had gone through a tripwire that shut down the entire operation. When the lifts stopped, there was total silence, and everyone on the slopes looked up to see the cause – a man dressed in white like the Pillsbury Doughboy swaying in the wind. The tableau I viewed below was reminiscent of Dosso Dossi's painting of *The Ascension*. I jostled some more until the leather straps around my wrist finally slipped over my hand. That was followed by a rapid descent.

The descent was not going to be a piece of cake. I was ten feet in the air with six-foot extensions on my feet. It's not like I could just hit and roll; it's not like I couldn't get entangled in my skis like a pretzel. But I had no time to think as I dropped from the sky. Somehow, some way, in a gymnastic move that I could never repeat – I STUCK IT. My knees gave, jarred by the landing, but they didn't give. The tableau changed to the same scene except with all mouths open. Then, I raised my arms as if I had dismounted from the uneven parallel bars. The gawkers burst into an explosion of applause, hoots, hollers, and laughter.

I took off my skis, and never put them on again (when I say *never,* I mean to this day). For the rest of the trip, you could find me in front of the open-hearth fireplace in the lobby, contemplating my escape from the jaws of death. Oh, yes, I was mercilessly teased and laughed at. But nothing could destroy my peace of mind as I sat with a mug of hot buttered rum and a body still whole.

Once a Time a Pawn

Galen Keen was smug about his knowledge and rationality. He was pure science, and the role of the humanities in education befuddled him. The only relationship he had with the eternal verities is what could be measured. Intangibles like emotions, ethics, archetypes, and values were outside the orbit of his ego.

As a teacher of chemistry and physics, he was well suited to be sponsor of the chess club. The permutations of the chess pieces were like the combinatorial possibilities of the periodic table. Mr. Keen had an adoring young group of chess buffs, who in many ways were little mimeographs of their chess master. They saw themselves as extremely intelligent with IQs far above the "proletariat" of the school.

I had had some of these chess wunderkinder in my classes and, while they were good students, they had tolerant smiles on their faces as I tried to explain the multiple interpretations of a poem. "Multiple interpretations?" they would ask. "Surely, you jest, Mr. Settle. There can be only one interpretation and that is how the author meant it." They didn't like the idea that H_2o in literature could stand for rebirth, purity, fertility, death, creation, the feminine, etc. Much too inaccurate and irrelevant for their blood. But they parroted back whatever they needed to in order to get the good grade.

I did like Galen Keen, even though he was a bit pompous. We had overlapping interests in Isaac Asimov and Arthur C. Clarke, both as science popularizers and science-fiction writers. Then too, we liked to discuss the debate in psychology between B.F. Skinner and Carl Rogers, the former a behaviorist and the latter a client-centered therapist. These two approaches to psychology had all kinds of implications for education and literary interpretation. As you would expect, Galen favored the rat-in-the-maze studies of Skinner. Thus, despite our differences, we were friends, although friends in a rarefied atmosphere. My best friends usually were not quite as stiff as Galen, and at times, although well-educated, tended toward the wild and bawdy. I could not imagine going out and getting tipsy with Mr. Keen.

And it came to pass that one day after school, I went to the library to return some books. Galen was there with his team with a whiteboard full of chess moves. They were preparing for a big tournament in the state's capital. Our chess team was quite formidable and was among the elite in the state. Mr. Keen was getting them pumped up like a football coach, trying to get them to show confidence and even disdain in facing their opponents.

That's when I should have shut my mouth, but I didn't. "Ah, Mr. Keen, nothing I like better than chess buffs boasting in an open foyer." A malapropism that I had heard from a joke.

"Mr. Settle, I'm glad you dropped by. We don't need a malaprop, but we could use a prop. I'd like to demonstrate to the lads how they should face their opponents – their body postures and the fix of their eyes. Are you game?"

"The game's afoot," I replied, in my best Sherlockian accent.

He arranged a chessboard on a small table with two chairs facing one another. He had me take a position and a pose in one chair, while he demonstrated how the opposition should face his opponent in the other.

"You want me to be Boris Spassky or Bobby Fischer?" I joked.

"Just be serious and disdainful, Settle – *if* you can handle that."

I got myself into a condescending and stone-faced attitude as Keen took the chair opposite me.

Next, he said, "Mr. Settle, have you ever played chess? Because I would like to demonstrate how professionals move pieces and make eye contact."

I kept to my role, "Not only have I played chess, but I seriously don't believe that you can beat me."

Galen smirked, and said, "Mr. Settle, not only will I beat you, but I will annihilate you in a matter of minutes."

I could see the chess club members being drawn into our exchanges. They tightened ranks around the table to get a better view.

"Let's allow our play do the talking, Chess Coach of mere neophytes. Make your move."

I seldom took my eyes off Keen as we moved our pieces. I had no strategies at all, except to stay in character and play wildly. When Keen made a move, I commented, "Now *that* was a mistake." Quickly, I responded with a move that defied logic. "That should get your small mind working, Mr. Keen, or should I say, Mr. Dull."

We continued briskly back and forth, both of us keeping defiant postures as we traded wilting barbs. It was over in eight moves – "Checkmate," I proclaimed.

The students were stunned. Galen must have looked at the board for five minutes before he accepted the fact that he had been defeated. I got up regally from my chair and left the group in total silence.

Somehow, someway, I had played my pieces so erratically that it had caught Galen off guard. No one was more shocked than I was when I saw the opening to the king after a handful of moves. Pure, unadulterated luck. Galen sent a messenger ten minutes later to my classroom to ask for a rematch. I told the messenger that it was a waste of my time. I had other more complex activities to attend to.

Thus, I had established myself as a chess genius. The chess club students looked at me in a reverent way after that. Of course, Keen was desperate for a rematch over the next months, but I always refused. Sometimes I played him like a trout, giving him a moment of hope that I actually was considering a rematch, but then I would withdraw the bait. His club members wanted to see a rematch, but I'd always tell them, "I'd consider doing it if I hadn't beaten Mr. Keen so badly, but I dare not humiliate him again. He has gone through enough suffering as it is."

You would be wrong if you thought I was a good enough person to let Galen off the hook. I kept up the charade as a chess guru until the day I moved on to another school. As far as I was concerned, the gods that Galen eschewed had used me as their instrument to punish him for his hubris. Checkmate, mere mortal.

Daddy's Girl

René Goodwin was dependable in every way – she was a good student, but not a top student; she was shy, but not to the point that she wouldn't comment in class; she was normal looking but didn't try to use make-up or clothes to be more attractive. She was a quiet presence that did what she was supposed to without any demands for special attention.

There was one area that she was particularly good at, though – she was a track star. She was persistent in becoming a highly ranked runner in our area. I witnessed her often staying after track practice to get in a few more reps in the running events at which she excelled. Even from a distance, I could tell it was René on the track because of a figure always shadowing her, her father.

René had a very close relationship with her father. For some reason that I never knew, her mother was absent from the family. I assumed she had either died or abandoned the family. Her dad was her single parent. In addition, Mr. Goodwin was Minister Goodwin, the leader of a local Baptist church. When you would see the two of them together, love ricocheted back and forth with palpable sparks. René was a Daddy's girl that was not only enamored by love for her father as a parent but also by the respect for what her father represented to the community – a stalwart of Christian kindness and morality.

Then, on a weekend during her senior year, the headlines of the paper blasted out, "**Minister Arrested for Sex with Children**." Oh my god! The minister was Charles Goodwin. The lurid details of his sexual liaisons with boys and girls from his congregations filled the first and second pages of the newspaper. Soon the TV networks chimed in adding to the shock waves. Minster Goodwin's face appeared in newspapers around the nation.

When I met with my colleagues in the lounge Monday morning, we could talk of nothing else. But our main concern was for René. What was this going to do to René! We all knew how much she admired her father. She had to be devastated! We wondered where she would be staying and if we could get some message to her about how sorry we were for her. We'd be willing to do anything to keep her abreast of assignments if she so desired. She needn't have to come back to school.

As I was making my way to my first-period class, I heard a hush and saw students moving up against their lockers to form an open pathway. Making her way to my class, head down and shoulders slumped, was René. She had chosen to show up rather than forego the humiliation and gossip that surrounded her because of her father. It took no mind reader to tell she was in the throes of deep despair and despondency. It silenced everyone as she sat in the back of the class with her head on the desk, tears moistening the sleeves of her sweater. I have never witnessed a braver act.

She appeared the next day and the next. She didn't miss a day or an assignment until she finished her senior year: a feat far greater than any race that she would ever run. That she was a changed person there could be no doubt – she smiled less, and her writing became more profound. She never went out for track again, but you could see a determination that would lead her into loftier pursuits in the future.

All of us were humbled by her courage, and I remember how we all applauded and cheered as she walked up in cap and gown to receive her diploma in the absence of her father. We all knew that René Goodwin would save us someday when we ourselves were faced with tragedy and looked for inspiration in a story of resilience. I know I thought about her as I was going through a depression after my divorce and really did not want to show up for school. But I thought, if René could do it, so could I.

Last Child in the Woods

A gender bias that I faced throughout my Jurassic career was that if you were male you were qualified to coach. Now I'm not talking about coaching the main meal sports like varsity football or basketball. I'm referring to side dishes like fifth or sixth-grade track coach, freshman basketball assistant, bowling sponsor, etc. Therefore, I wasn't surprised when I arrived at Jefferson High School that I was unceremoniously given the title of Cross Country Coach.

I never winced or protested for a second, even though I had never done any long-distance running, except during basic training in the army. Why squirm when I knew I could not fail as a coach – the school was only looking for a body, albeit a male body, to cover the activities of a required but unpopular sport. None of the really good athletes in the high school "went out for" (more precisely "showed up for") cross-country.

As I looked over the variety of bodies that "showed up" for cross-country the following spring, the future of the team didn't look too promising. It was a motley crew ranging from short chubby to tall gangly, from mismatched socks to combat boots, from red-necked farm kids to sedentary, pasty intellectuals. There was no sleek thoroughbred among them. What demon had possessed them to go out for a grueling sport like cross-country, I had no idea. Maybe they all thought they had the will necessary for long-distance, even though they couldn't come up with the grace necessary for basketball or the brutality necessary for football.

My plan for their training was simple. This high school was in the sticks, or more accurately the corn stalks. There was a back road connecting the high school with the middle school that was about eight miles long. It was fairly level and cut right through acres of Illinois topsoil. That meant, of course, no trees and no shade because farmers farmed right up to the road's edge. The road was paved with asphalt that baked in the sun, adding another five to ten degrees to the ambient temperature. Every day after school for the running season, I met them in front of the school, had them stretch out, line up, and then take off to the sound of my whistle. After that, there was no strategy. Their job was simply to make it to the middle school running, jogging, walking, or crawling.

Did I run with them? Of course not! I hated running long distances. But I did bring a bicycle to school so that I could ride up and down the long line of gasping runners and provide them with encouragement. Also, I provided them with water, which I always carried in a backpack full of canteens (there was no bottled water at the time). I had to make sure none of them got dehydrated or overheated. At the end of their eight miles, I made sure there was a cooler full of cold soda to greet them under a shade tree in front of the middle school.

This is where Thomas (not Tom) Jillings enters the story. We never waited for Thomas Jillings to finish. We always had to pick him up in the van on the way back to the high school. On a team with the worst runners in the county, Jillings was the worst runner. Being short and pudgy without a smidgen of muscle tone, he was not built for long-distance. His combed-over blond hair hung over his eyes as he ran, and I was worried about him blindly stepping in front of a truck. I had tried to give him as many options as I could so that he could hang up his sneakers gracefully, but he was dogged about facing a physical challenge in his life. For him, it was a rite of passage into manhood.

After a few weeks, I saw progress in all my runners. Their times were definitely improving, and even Jillings made it back to thunderous applause before the van headed back. I was actually encouraged that we would not make asses of ourselves in our first meet that was coming up in a few days.

Cross-country meets in rural areas definitely have those pastoral sights, sounds, and smells associated with living in the country. Our first meet was on a course laid out through a series of pastures and woods. Cattle were grazing and bawling, and there was plenty of cow manure to keep runners dancing along their way. Also, there was the danger of antagonistic bulls to watch out for. The terrain was rough and would not have met the specifications of urban cross-country regulations. The course was not for the weak-ankled. Furrows and dirt clods made "clodhoppers" a relevant term. The trails through the woods were narrower than they should be for passing another runner, and hidden tree roots and stones were waiting to bring down the unsuspecting runner.

But despite all, it was a beautiful spring day with abundant yellows from dandelions and field mustards. With a cooling breeze and a 70-degree temperature, the day was ideal for a long, sweaty run. The team was ready, and they loosened up as they gathered at the starting line. When the signal was given, they bolted off like a cluster of wildebeests, but as they circled the pasture and entered the woods, they elongated into a line with each runner establishing his own pace and position. Now all the coaches had to do was sit in lawn chairs and wait with stopwatches and clipboards.

All the courses on our cross-country circuit were between three to seven miles. This particular course was a long one, being six miles. Close to an hour later, runners began trickling in at a moderate rate. Then there was an onslaught of runners coming out of the forest with their coaches shouting at them to make a final burst to overtake the runners in front of them. Finally, there was a dribble of the slowest runners, some staggering and some walking with hands on their sides to the chalk line.

"Is that the last of them, Coach?" asked the opposing coach, as one of my kids staggered out of the woods an hour and a half later. "No, we got one more out there," I said with a bit of embarrassment.

An hour and a half stretched into two hours. The officials and opposing team had already gathered up all their equipment and were sitting impatiently on their bus ready to leave. Sheepishly, I said, "Thomas is a little slow. He should be here any minute." (I had my fingers crossed behind me.)

Two hours stretched into two and fifteen minutes, then to two and a half. The waiting was over. We had to go get him because it was getting dark.

Armed with flashlights, both teams entered the course at different places, hoping we could meet later with Thomas Jillings in tow. The woods reverberated with the shouts of Thomas's name. After an hour, nothing. It was dark now. Dark in a way that only the country can get with no ambient light from houses or streetlights. What to do?

I told the other team that they should go. I would take care of this. With both concern and embarrassment, I drove to the nearest farmhouse (there were no cell phones) and called the superintendent:

"Ah, um, Sir, I know it's late, but we've lost Thomas Jillings at the cross-country meet."

"Lost him! How in the hell can you lose him! There's nothing out there."

"Well, he just didn't return after the race was over. We combed the woods and pastures looking for him. Now it's too dark to do anything. What do you think we should do?"

"God, Settle. You do keep things lively at a school. I'll have someone call the parents to come pick up their kids, and then I'll call Vern and get out the local volunteer fire department. They should have the equipment for some kind of search."

With fire department and police sirens, bullhorns and shouts, we did not awaken Thomas Jillings. He had covered quite a bit of territory, more than the six miles of the course. Early in the race, he had gotten lost because Thomas was always so far behind in a race that there was no one in front of him to follow. Pair this with the fact that he ran with his head down and hair in his eyes, so it was easy for him to miss a marker.

Mistakenly, he got derailed by deer paths and streambeds before it occurred to him in his trudging, blind gait something was amiss. Panic and fear set in? No way for the boy with an iron will and facile intellect. He wandered for a while until he found a place to spend the night.

The place was an abandoned family cemetery behind a wrought iron fence covered in vines. We found Jillings at about four in the morning, curled up fast asleep beneath an angel on a tombstone. Unafraid, he had slept the sleep of the dead because it took a while to arouse him, and then he was confused about the fact he was being rescued.

When we came out of the woods, his parents were waiting frantically for their only boy (spoiled boy, I might add). Immediately, Thomas's mother chastised me for losing her boy, while the father shut up as he was trained to do. For Thomas Jillings, this was going to be his last hurrah toward manliness in high school. He would never be the last child in the woods again. Mom put an end to his "silly" pursuit of cross-country racing. And it was back to the books for Thomas. And for me, it solved the problem of some very late practices and very late meets. Yet, I felt sorry for Thomas Jillings, and I hoped someday he would break away from his mother and become the man he wanted to be.

Conclusion: The Positive Side of Negative

"That which does not kill us makes us stronger." I don't know if I entirely agree with this quote from Nietzsche, but I do know that surviving Great Awk moments can be turned into positives. The strategy that I've developed over time is to take my asinine moves in life and turn them into humor. It's a tenet that has become a dogma in my life: people relate better to your admissions of being a fool than to your pretenses of having some kind of perfection. When you put your fragilities out there for others to see, it's amazing how fast people accept you and empathize with you.

Certainly, René Goodwin's exposing her despair to the whole student body made us love her all the more. For Thomas Jillings, who had acquired the reputation of the boy who could sleep anywhere, his taking the kidding in good stride gave him some notoriety outside of academics that he had always wanted. With Galen Keen, his soundly being defeated by a seemingly inept chess player knocked him off his pedestal as a chess god. It's difficult to keep up the façade of a god, and I believe the wound that I gave him healed in a way that made him more relaxed and approachable to the students of the chess club. What about the man who hung by one arm from the ski tow rope? What did he learn? Well, he decided to be content on the bunny slopes of life. There is no shame in staying at the level of your abilities if you can walk away with your legs still intact.

Chapter 10
Loungevity

In the marathon of a teaching career, I don't know how I would have survived without the laughter, affection, renewal, stories, and strategies that I found with fellow colleagues in the teachers' lounge. Working with students all the livelong day can be like Jane Goodall spending the days with chimps – you long for adult conversation; you need a break lest your anger and frustration get the better of you. How I sometimes longed to get away from the classroom to cuss, to vent, to be silly, to smoke, to drink coffee, and to gossip. The high school teachers' lounge was the place I could do this. Teachers have as much of a need for a peer group as do adolescents.

More education occurs in teachers' lounges than I could have ever imagined. How many times in my early career was I taken aside and told to put on hold what I had learned in my education classes and do things in a different way. How many times I was told how to deal with certain students, administrators, parents, and school boards. There was always a Yoda in the lounge telling me, "Marty, learn to use the force."

I would like to think as the years passed that I became that arm around the shoulder of many new teachers helping them along the difficult path of the dark forces within the system. There are so many unnecessary roadblocks put in the way of being a good educator. The faculty lounge was the place during the Jurassic that I found that I could face and overcome those roadblocks.

Initiation

"Something there is that doesn't love a wall" (Robert Frost) or in my case a closed door. Something that makes us want to try the handle and peek in. If the door is labeled "Keep Out," the temptation is amplified. I suppose this desire is as old as Eden. One of the doors in my high school student days that I wanted to go behind was labeled "Faculty Lounge." What did teachers do in there? What did they say? How did they act in the presence of their peers? This curiosity was like trying to see what Hollywood actors were like when they were not on screen. After all, being a teacher is a kind of performance profession.

When this door first opened up to me, I was doing my student teaching, and I was a senior in college. My mentoring teacher (the subject of Ch.1 of this book) was Miss Boltz, and it was she who took me through the sacred portal for the first time. I look back and consider this moment a rite of passage – I was entering into the world of the elders. And what did I see?

First of all, I saw those vigilant enforcers of the nonsmoking code, smoking themselves to oblivion. Mr. Deters, a dapper man and a history teacher, had a cigarette hanging out of his mouth like a New York cabby. Another matronly woman, a model of primness and propriety, had taken off her granny shoes and was wriggling toes in nylon stocking on the coffee table. Ties were loosened, and diet coke cans and coffee cups littered the room in various stages of decay. Newspapers with articles torn out for class use were strewn beneath couches and on the floor.

Miss Boltz introduced me to the denizens who lodged here during my free period. Oddly enough, one of them was a former high school teacher of mine who had transferred to this particular school.

"How do you do, Mr. Cudney. Remember me?"

"Why it's Marty Settle! Can it be that long ago? It seems like only yesterday that I caught you cheating on a final exam, didn't I?"

"I was hoping you'd forgotten that, Mr. Cudney."

"Ah, spilt milk under the bridge, my boy. And call me Bob. You're one of us now."

"Okay, B-Bob."

One of us now? OMG! I had gone over to the dark side, a prey to a predator! The faculty lounge was a transforming ritual of consciousness. I had now put on the robe of the secret society of teachers. I would now be known as "Mr. Settle."

Avalon

Why a lounge for teachers? Isn't their job easy enough as it is? I think many have no imagination about what it's like being a high school teacher on a daily basis. The stresses and energy necessary to engage this developmental group far outweigh the business of organizing classes, preparing classes, and grading papers.

To come under the icy scrutiny of high school students week after week is to come under the eye of the diamond cutter. Each facet of your personality is subject to a severe magnification, and then the chisel comes down on the fault lines. I have come under such scrutiny. I have had students keep track of every "ya know" I said in class. Over the years, I have acquired a series of nicknames – "Brillo" for my wiry hair, "Spock" for my pointed ears, and "GQ" for my inability to match my clothes.

Once I did an exercise in my speech class. Each student had to imitate through body language one of the other members of the class, while the rest of us were to guess who it was. No words were allowed, just facial expressions and gestures. One student came to the front of the class and hoisted up his pants. "Mr. Settle," the class immediately shouted. What! I do that? Indeed, as I began to monitor myself, I found that I did do that exact gesture as I began a class.

I have had my laugh imitated with unerring accuracy. I have had my manhood impugned – what kind of a sissy boy would become an English teacher? I've had my own words thrown back in my face. I've been humbled in my contradictions ("Do I contradict myself? Very well, I contradict myself, I am large, I contain multitudes." Walt Whitman). I have had my jokes and humor fall as flat as roadkill.

Students can be merciless in their judgments and as surgical as tarantula wasps. Yet, I didn't blame them. I, too, had my teenage years where the hypocrisy of the adult world deserved my disdain. Unfortunately, teens, unlike adults, cannot look back and see their own folly. To be a teacher one must have skin as thick as a rhino's. This is the law of the jungle for any aspiring secondary educator. Sensitive types should seek out another profession because if you think students will be considerate of your needs, think again. Not only will students not have compassion for you as a teacher, but they will enjoy your demise. Some classes will joyfully tell you about the teachers they have driven out of the profession.

Then there is the relentless world of discipline. Most jobs in the world other than the military have little to do with enforcing discipline. Yet every day, we teachers are charged with keeping the unstable chemistries of adolescents from acting up or out. Teachers must be constantly worried about staying in control and keeping people on task. I remember when I first began teaching college. The saints in heaven be praised! It was like taking off a heavy layer of armor. You mean there's no sending students to the principal's office; there are no parents to call; there's no keeping the disrupters after school. You mean students in general aren't discipline problems because they don't have to come to class if they don't want to, and all I have to do is record their absences and take it off their grade – no questions asked. I remember talking with another colleague in college who transitioned from high school to college like I did. We both felt that somehow, we were pulling a fast one on the university because everything was so easy.

The faculty room at the university was a luxury and not a necessity, while the faculty lounge on the high school level was not a luxury but a necessity. In order to suffer the slings and arrows of outrageous fortune as a high school teacher, I often staggered to that island of sanity that was the faculty lounge. It was here I could relax, complain, share, and vent. And then when I returned to class, my heart had been given:

A change of mood
And saved some part
Of a day I had rued.
　　　　　　— Robert Frost

Boiler Room and beyond

My first faculty lounge as a full-time teacher was in a boiler room. You had to go down a set of rickety stairs and then turn on the single bulb that hung from the ceiling to expose a little corner called the "Faculty Ritz." The lounge consisted of a couch that the Salvation Army wouldn't have taken, three rusted folding chairs, and a wire spool table with ashtrays that fit in the holes. Since the ashtrays were only emptied once a millennium, a lingering smell of ashes always hung in the air.

And yet, it had warmth both physical and psychological. Being next to the boiler, we got an additional helping of heat. The flames from the boiler were visible, which created an ambience of coziness. On some wintery days when the heating system could not warm the classrooms above, the boiler room's heat and the mesmerizing flames made it difficult to leave the glow of the conversation and cigarettes.

As I moved to other schools and to faculty lounges that were less grungy, I found that in essence, they were all pretty much the same. We were all in combat situations, and we were all soldiers sharing foxhole pedagogies. But we shared much more: we shared our relationships with spouses and dating companions, the stress of caretaking a parent, money problems, politics, and religion. We shared jokes and vented over both students and administrators. Negotiating new contracts was particularly stressful, as we lined up and took sides with union versus non-union. But most of all we gossiped.

Two things you could count on when you opened the door and entered the faculty lounge: smoke that would exit as if the place were on fire; gossip that would be spreading as fast as fire. Not all teachers came to the lounge – some because of the smoking, but most because of the gossip, which they found unconscionable.

Gossip is a word that thoughtlessly is always given a negative connotation. First of all, there's a misogynistic component that attributes this behavior to busybody women, who have nothing better to do. Usually, this kind of gossip is trite. Then, there is the other kind of communal gossip that can be hurtful and vicious. With that in mind, however, many psychologists and social scientists today have not only indicated positive values for gossip but have downright claimed its social necessity. "Gossip is what makes human society as we know it possible," is a claim by evolutionary psychologist Robin Dunbar. The good of gossip is that it improves the bonds and cooperation between gossipers and, as one study concluded, it is a means to learn about cultural norms and a way to assess one's social standing.

Without having the benefit of current studies, I instinctively knew that the gossip in the lounge had positive benefits. Oh, there were always a few cynical teachers that I ignored. Whatever had twisted their hearts and let them dry out I wasn't about to probe. They had their say, and then their bile was passed over. But the majority of the stories were enlightening, humorous, salacious, and defusing.

I know that there were many times that I came into the faculty lounge on the verge of strangling a student. My mood was read quickly and, once I confessed my problem, it was pored over by similar experiences, possible solutions, and a heavy helping of confirmation that I wasn't alone in these feelings.

The same was true in the other direction when we were amazed by the accomplishments and integrity of a student. I remember one student in particular who had four older brothers whose history in our school was one of thugs and drugs. We all had experiences in teaching the brothers, and we expected little variation on a theme when the fifth brother came into the system. However, much to our constant amazement, David Jenkins was an honor roll student, a guard on the basketball team, and a model of good behavior. We mulled over this mystery with all the questions used in a 5Ws and an H writing assignment: who, what, where, when, why, and how. And we continued to pore over the enigma of David after he left us to attend college.

Administrators, colleagues, and school boards provided us with many rounds of discussion. Everyone was scrutinized closely, and we all knew intimately the hypocrisies, strengths, victories, defeats, and humiliations of this set of people. Personally, I was very happy to be the subject of gossip during my year of separation and divorce. It was a time in my life that I went through a depression and could barely get out of bed to come to school each day. I can't say I taught my best during that year, and it was easy to see the dark circles under my eyes. Yet the support and understanding for my situation came directly from the lounge circle. They had my back, and their affection was palpable.

Did my lounge mates talk about my weaknesses and annoying qualities? You betcha. But then, so do my wife and daughter. I've learned a lot (sometimes painfully) from both.

Steering Committees

Many things are steered from the faculty lounge: all the way from new course offerings to sexual behavior. The agendas of these "committee" meetings in the lounge were quite informal. Someone might say (as really did happen) that the poet W.S. Merwin was giving a reading at a university nearby. Before you could say "free verse," plans were laid down on how to get a bus, substitutes, money, and the principal's permission to get some of our classes to attend the reading.

New courses were birthed in the lounge. Once I nonchalantly said as yearbook sponsor wouldn't it be great if we could develop our own pictures. In the following months through the assistance and cooperation of all sorts of people, we had commandeered an old storage room and converted it into a photo lab. The eventual goal was to make photography a class that students on the yearbook staff could get credit for and then expand this offering through our art department. The principal got on board pretty quickly when he realized the total cost of the lab would be 100 dollars and that other schools in the district would pay to bus students in to take photography classes.

Another area that the lounge steering committee excelled in was raising money. To be a member of the faculty lounge was to make sure you had a bunch of ones in your wallet. You would always be tapped for a dollar or two for one of the other teachers' fundraisers or pet projects: the library needed books, drama wanted a spotlight, the band needed new uniforms, poor students needed supplies, etc. There was never enough money from the localities and the states to provide for all the needs of the school. Often the faculty took it upon themselves to raise the necessary monies.

The plans on how to raise the money came from ingenious contributions from many in the lounge. Most projects were fun along with being profitable. Once we had a putt-putt golf tournament over the weekend. The holes for the course were set up in the hallways and classrooms. There was plenty of natural roll in the hallways and plenty of natural hazards in the classrooms where most of the holes were located. After collecting the entry fees, we had a hefty amount of money for both the fundraising cause and cash awards to the winners. Further, this event brought students, parents, faculty, administrators, and the community together for a delightful weekend activity. As you would expect, the teachers put in a lot of time without recompense.

Did I say earlier (and without a moment of explanation) that the steering committee dealt with sexual behavior? You read right. The unacceptable was not the unspeakable to us of the Jurassic. We were very aware that there were dangerous sexual waters between a faculty member (usually male) and a student (usually female). Of course, this was an unequal relationship that could not be tolerated in any form. Yet, knowing the power of sex, we were realistic enough to know that occasionally teachers were subjected to this kind of temptation.

If we observed a faculty member getting a bit too cozy with a student, we pointed this out to him (as I said, it was almost always a male) in no uncertain terms. If he thought that there was a possibility that what was happening was going unnoticed, that there weren't rumors flying around, or that he could be secretive enough to not get caught, he was quickly informed in the lounge that the word was out, and it was time to back off before another misstep could mean the end to his career. We steered many illicit activities from occurring within the informal confines of the lounge.

Besides policing ourselves in these sexual matters, we were also a fount of information on how to avoid any awkward sexual allegations or situations. There were a whole host of unwritten rules that we promulgated. For instance, one rule that often complicated my life but was totally necessary was "Never give an individual student a ride home – male or female." There were many evenings when I had worked late with students, rehearsing a play or putting together a yearbook. Because of some unforeseen circumstance, it would often end up that somebody did not have a ride home. Both the student and I were tired and wanted to get home. It would have saved a lot of time for the student and for me if I just drove him or her home. But in these pre-cell phone times, I had to go to the office and use the telephone to muster up a parent or relative or neighbor to come and pick up Sally or Bob. Sometimes, I was forced to take the janitor with me and then bring him back to school. But these kinds of restrictions were well worth it in the long run with – no gossip, no temptations, no unforeseen misperceptions.

A Ripple in Time

I recall a time when one of our faculty members, who had been with us for around five years, left the system to go on to more composted pastures. This was not, of course, unusual because teachers would always be leaving the system to improve their situations. What was unusual about Mr. Tomkins leaving was that he was never mentioned again. It was as if he were one of those non-persons of communist Russia, whose names and pictures were taken out of all records. However, unlike the non-persons, Tomkins was not expunged intentionally. It's just he had always kept aloof from the faculty community because he was too busy in his many entrepreneurial activities to give anyone the time of day. Since he had never been present for us, his absence never created the slightest ripple in the space-time continuum of our school narrative.

Later, when I came to this realization that his absence meant nothing, I had an epiphany of how horrible it would be for me when I left, if I were not part of the future narrative of the faculty lounge. The faculty lounge is the campfire where teachers gather and recount the exploits of their ancestral past. When you join a lounge, you become initiated into a history that is before your time. It becomes a goal to be later incorporated into the litany of famous warriors of past history:

"Do you remember when Mr. Barkley came to school drunk, and we covered every one of his classes? Principal

Dobbins never knew he hadn't shown up for one of his classes and was sleeping it off in the faculty lounge."

"Anyone know what happened to Hope Sheridan? Now there was a character. She was from the Ozark hills and chewed tobacco instead of smoking. She always kept a spitting cup in here – nasty thing. Hope was tougher than wang leather [you tell me where that expression comes from]. Nearly knocked the head off of our All-State tackle Bobby Morris for making a sexual comment. Her handprint was on his face for the entire day."

"How about the 'Countessa,' Cheryl Geers? Hard to believe that a woman as beautiful as she could have such an intellectual side. And a wild side, too! Remember how she got drunk and then won a wet T-shirt contest at one of the local bars. Damn near got fired over that. Union lawyers saved her ass on that one."

My father always gave me the comforting advice when I worried over small things, "Marty, a hundred years from now no one will know the difference." I must agree he was right; most of us will go the way of obscurity after a century. But it's not a century that I want to be remembered – 25 to 30 years would satisfy me. And I have achieved that goal in some faculty lounges.

A few of my past colleagues are still alive and, if not kicking, at least tapping their toes in faculty lounges. They tell me I occasionally come up in the litany of remembrance of things past:

"Do you remember the time Mr. Settle used to re-write the principal's quotes of the day? It was hilarious, and Principal Haggard never caught on. Of course, he was an idiot."

"Embarrassing. I'll tell you em-bare-ass-ing. We had a teacher here, Mr. Settle, who would always do handstands on his desk. One time he came down slowly from a handstand and ripped out the back of his pants. He taught all day with his back to the wall."

"I'll tell you one of the best plays we ever put on in this school – it was a melodrama (I can't remember the name of it now) but it was put on by the senior class. Marty Settle and Beth Merriman directed it; it was a musical. Some of the most unlikely of our seniors were in it. Not top students by any stretch of the imagination. You wouldn't believe the talent that was hidden in the ranks of these 'sweathog' seniors. They sang, danced, and acted beyond anything you would expect."

That stories about me that continued to leaven the narratives of faculty lounges 30 years later brought me a sense of completion that surpasseth all understanding. It is total fulfillment for a long teaching career. And if in years to come I can continue to provide a laugh, an insight, an excitement, or an inspiration to future teachers in faculty lounges, it would be all the immortality I could ever desire.

Conclusion: Losing Your Faculties

"And so, if I were not president but king in America, I would abolish all teachers' lounges where they sit together and worry about how 'woe is us.'" Ohio Governor John Kasich received quite a bit of flak from teachers for that statement in 2015.

First of all, if we do spend some time in the faculty lounge worrying about our futures, what's the problem there? I suppose Gov. Kasich doesn't worry about being re-elected. Teachers are no different from most citizens in society –we are concerned about our incomes and our abilities to support our families in the future.

Secondly, the faculty lounge is not a place of laziness and complaint. Call it the faculty "room" instead if it helps to change your perceptions. The faculty room is the hub of professional connectivity and collaboration. It should be a place that educational systems not only allow but cultivate for the good of the entire system. To eliminate them would be to cripple a valuable resource. What Kasich suggested just underlines a belief that I firmly hold – most politicians don't know a damn thing about education.

Finally, in the current climate of teacher employment, teachers are leaving the profession in droves. There are many reasons for this – pay being the most prominent. However, there are other factors that can make teaching a dignified profession worthy of a lifetime of devotion. One of them is treating teachers as professionals.

Ever since No Child Left Behind, I have seen a steady decline in the autonomy of teachers. What has happened over the years is that in spite of all their training and expertise, teachers are given less and less responsibility for the content of their classes and the shaping of their school's educational goals. Phrases like "teaching for the test" have taken away a lot of approaches and solutions that teachers as professionals could apply. Two other words that disturb me are *accountability* and *efficiency*. These words signal to me a mistrust in teachers' abilities to manage themselves, which is the number one attribute of a professional.

If you want to retain teachers, you have to give them a greater participation in formulating the curriculum and measuring the results in their particular classes and schools. To take away faculty lounges or the time to go to faculty lounges is a restriction that forbids the collegiality necessary for professionals. It's no surprise to me many teachers are leaving the "profession." They don't have the basic respect due to professionals. This requirement is beyond money and must be an imperative if teachers are going to be retained.

Can I hear an "Amen"?

Chapter 11
The Good, the Bad, and the Beautiful

"I liked the company of most of my colleagues, who were about equally divided among good men who were good teachers, awful men who were awful teachers, and the grotesques and misfits who drift into teaching and are so often the most educative influences a boy meets in school. If a boy can't have a good teacher, give him a psychological cripple or an exotic failure to cope with; don't just give him a bad, dull teacher. This is where the private schools score over state-run schools; they can accommodate a few cultured madmen on the staff without having to offer explanations."

— Robertson Davies, *Fifth Business*

I do believe that misfits of one sort or another drift into the teaching business. There can be many reasons for this: exotic personalities that won't fit into other professions; psychologically or socially wounded people that like the safety of the classroom's controlled environment; or people that fit into the old dictum (mostly false): those that can, do; those that can't, teach. Whatever the reason for these misfits, as Robertson Davies points out in his novel, they don't have to be a bad thing for students or the school.

During the looseness of the Jurassic, it was easier for these outliers to hide out in the public educational systems. I will give you a thumbnail of three of these that I came across in my years of teaching. All three of them would be fired today. *And yet*...they had something of value to offer students – and we can speculate whether our educational system is diminished today without a few of them around.

The Good

If ever a person's body reflected his or her psychological state, then Henry McFadden's did. He swelled with great disappointment in his marriage, his children, and his status in life. He was disappointed in his students, other faculty members, the administration, the school board, his classroom equipment – the weather, for god's sake. There was not a positive topic that you could approach McFadden with that he couldn't turn into a negative. And so, he ate huge quantities of food as his only comfort in life and grew into a hulk of over three hundred pounds.

He was the saddest man I ever knew. What white whale had bitten off a piece of his heart, I never found out. But I did see pictures of him as a young man – handsome, athletic, smiling, and slim. Apparently, at one time in his life, he was brimming with optimism and potential. At one time in his life, he was a successful biologist with a shining future. Then, there must have come a crushing blow of either event or chemistry or both.

School was Henry McFadden's place of escape. He was the first to arrive in the morning and the last to leave at night. He usually spent the entire day behind a long table in the biology lab. I never saw him eat in his classroom or in the cafeteria. He never appeared in the faculty lounge. And during the summer? Yep, you could expect him to be the only teacher in the school, working in his classroom, cleaning biology equipment, studying new materials, and taking care of the aquarium. Obviously, he avoided being at home with his wife and three children, who, I could tell, suffered greatly because of his remoteness.

And yet...despite the hugeness of his depression, Henry McFadden was a great teacher. His great dissatisfaction with life was mostly hidden from students, and they benefited from the only place in his existence that he could escape to besides food. The energies he bottled up to stay away from home or to go out into the wider world exploded in the classroom. He was a tough and respected teacher. The administration allowed him all his idiosyncrasies, including never showing up for meetings to slamming recalcitrant students up against the wall, because they knew they were paying one teacher who was doing the work of two. Students from McFadden's class were always winning academic scholarships in biology. All his students were well prepared for college, and many students, because of McFadden, majored in biology.

You can always tell a great teacher when you see how many of his or her students return to visit after they graduate. Henry always had a flock of these, much to the chagrin of many of us "normal" teachers. He was loved, even though he did not love himself. He was even thanked by the students that he had manhandled. Imagine that.

As you might expect given his weight, Henry McFadden did not live a long life. His predictable heart attack came, and he was gone. But he did create a vortex in the school, which nobody could fill. If I were a superstitious man, I could believe he still walks the school corridors at night and, on occasion, scares the hell out of some teacher who has to stay late or a suggestible janitor. All I know is that Henry McFadden took his great misery to the grave without revealing a smidgen of its origin. His great mystery created a misfit, who oddly had a profound effect on the lives of many students. *Requiescat in pace,* Henry.

The Bad

At the other end of the spectrum from Henry McFadden was the irrepressible Markley Ott or "The Otter" as we called him. Like McFadden, "The Otter" was disappointed in life, but his response was entirely different. He had a bounce in his step and a twinkle of mischief in his eye. He might have been disgusted with absurdities in education, politics, and people, but he found plenty in life (including pot and alcohol) to keep him amused.

As a fellow English teacher, I loved talking to Markley, who was intelligent and witty. I always considered myself well-read, but he out-read me two books to one. He was up on all the current literary authors, and he was always telling me I had to read this or that book so that we could discuss it. I could never keep up, but the books that we did read mutually provided material for interchanges during the 10-minute transitions between classes. Hallway duty wasn't so bad when I had Markley to talk to in a frothing sea of students.

You may be asking at this point, "What was the problem?" The problem was that "The Otter" was a child of the 60s like me. But unlike myself, he had not succumbed to an establishment existence. He was anti-authority, cynical, and immune to intimidation. Absurdity and irony informed his worldview. He was a nightmare to administrators, not only because he often didn't follow the rules, but because he *blatantly* didn't follow the rules.

I got my first sense of the man the moment we were introduced upon my arriving at a new job mid-semester. He was wearing a lab coat to class as if he were going to dissect a sentence using a scalpel. From my guide, I had heard that this was his usual attire. However, on this occasion, he had sewn to his lab coat unmatched socks and crumpled sheets of fabric softener. It seems the message that he was trying to convey to his students and to the world was the "importance" of stomping out "static cling." With tongue in cheek, he told me that "static cling" was an evil that our society should no longer have to endure and should be attacked with all the moral and economic resources that our society could muster. Other issues like poverty be damned. O-o-o-kay. I liked him right away.

In the traditional sense, he was not a good teacher. He dillydallied with a little reading here and a little writing there – loosely connected material on themes that interested him at the time, like static cling. I don't believe he took on anything as rigorous as grammar. He lacked conviction that any of this mattered in the long run for his students. He liked to use his class as a bully pulpit for criticism of the powers that be both in world politics and in our own school (the principal and superintendent received the brunt).

So why wasn't he fired? "The Otter" had a long history of administrations trying to fire him. When confrontation time came, he had an appetite for the fight, and he had a number of resources in his corner. First of all, he had a popularity in the community born of the fact he had coached a baseball team to a state championship. While Markley was not a good teacher, he was a good baseball coach, and he not only got notoriety for this but a lasting glory from supporters of school sports.

Secondly, there were always board members in his corner. He was a drinking buddy with a few and, when their loyalties between Budweiser and the school were challenged, they chose "the otter." He was a great guy to party with and, even though they knew his teaching skills were questionable, they wanted to begin their weekends with him presiding.

Finally, he belonged to the teachers' union, who brought in formidable lawyers that were ready for some serious and expensive litigation. Markley always came out on top – on top so often that as the years went by, superintendents and principals despaired of getting rid of him and resigned themselves to his unremitting shenanigans. Administrators came and went, but "The Otter" held steady.

And yet...students loved Markley Ott. As rebellious teenagers, they resonated with his rebellious nature and sarcastic humor. You would think his classes would be chaos, but *au contraire*. His classes were not undisciplined, even though they had plenty of downtime while Mr. Ott read the newspaper. No one wanted to come under the sting of his vitriolic tongue. Most sought his approval and, even though they, too, liked to defy the rules, they didn't want to cause trouble for the king of rule-breaking. They were his votaries.

Further, it's always great to be part of a legend. For instance, one spring day, when the weather had broken into shirtsleeve temperatures, I opened the windows of my classroom only to be accosted by the most delicious odors. The smells were coming from Mr. Ott's class next door. I leaned out the window because I heard a sizzling sound, and I beheld a Weber grill full of hot dogs and hamburgers standing next to Markley's window. Occasionally a student's arm would come out the window with a spatula to turn the burgers. This went on the entire day. "The Otter" had set up the grill, and his students provided buns, condiments, potato salad, and baked beans. Do you think any academic learning got done in Ott's classes that day? Do you think that his students had a story that would last them a lifetime? And, if you thought that the principal came around and shut the operation down, think again. It was "the otter," and "The Otter" was best ignored.

*And yet...*it is interesting for me to think about whether as an administrator, I would have fired Markley Ott. There was something about him that I thought was worthy of knowing and worthy of students being exposed to. I could have been resentful of "the otter's" freedom of cooking burgers while my class could only salivate to the smell as I was teaching them sonnet structure. But I was not. I truly got a kick out of his antics, and I thought we, as a school, would have been poorer for his absence. Would I want a school full of Markley Otts – a vision out of Hieronymus Bosch's hell? One misfit exotic was quite enough. But the value of having one exotic is like the king having his fool. The fool could make fun of the king without being beheaded, and he could defuse and amuse an authoritarian system. So, I'd let Markley keep his head while I and fellow teachers laughed our heads off.

The Beautiful

Tony Ricci was a physical specimen: handsome, 6 ft. 3, tanned, blond, blue-eyed with a body landscaped with muscles. He was an Adonis, but not an Apollo. Surrounding those strikingly blue eyes was the rest of the vacuum bulb. Ricci had, perhaps, the fewest wrinkles in his brain than any other teacher that I ever worked with.

It didn't bother me that he taught P.E. and driver's training – core courses for a football coach, which he was. However, I had some difficulties when he was assigned sections of American History classes. He had as about as much knowledge of American history as Sarah Palin had knowledge about Russia because she could see its shores from Alaska.

(Side note: Why is it that so many coaches have history minors and teach history classes in high school? Apparently, there is something I'm missing about the relationship between physical education and American history.)

Tony had a three-pronged approach to teaching history: 1. movies; 2. videotapes; and 3. guest speakers. With regard to movies and videotapes, he was indiscriminate about quality or appropriateness. *Gone with the Wind* covered the Civil War pretty well as far he was concerned, and *Kelly's Heroes* covered the essence of World War II. He darkened his classes so often to play media that he could have raised a variety of mushrooms on the side.

Because he so dominated the film and video equipment in the school, the librarian was forced to develop a system of timeshares so that the rest of the faculty could use the equipment fairly. With his back up against the wall, Tony broke down to buy his own equipment so that he was not put in the awkward position of having to actually talk to his class about American history. Finally, in the same thoughtless way, he would try to get guest speakers to come to his classes – World War II veterans, Daughters of the American Revolution, Native American artifact collectors, the local museum historians, elders of churches, etc. If you had any kind of brush with history, you were qualified to come and speak to Ricci's history classes.

One particular year, his third-period American history class funneled into my fourth-period freshman English class. Often, I got to hear tidbits of information that had come from Ricci's class during those rare moments when he was forced into some commentary about what his students had seen on TV. Usually, he ended up skewing the facts about history, whereby I would take a few minutes out at the beginning of my class to make some corrections.

For example, I found some kids talking about the Pulitzer Prize, except they were calling it the "Pearlitzer Surprise." "The what!" I said. It seems that's how Mr. Ricci pronounced it and understood it. Tony thought the recipient of the award was "surprised" to get it, and the recompense for the prize was not cash but pearls. Truly, I would like to tell you that I made this up to see if you were paying attention. Sadly, no.

Okay, I was exasperated with Mr. Ricci's poor teaching habits and total unfamiliarity with his teaching subject. But since it was general knowledge that he was inept as a history teacher (but a great football coach), I joined the silence and said nothing about it. I treated Tony well, although if I had chastised him, I wondered if he would have known the difference. He was about as literal as they come. If I would have told him to go fly a kite, it wouldn't have surprised me if he responded, "I love to fly kites." Sarcasm? Forget about sarcasm. Sarcasm would have been lost on Ricci as much as quantum physics. "Hey, Tony, I like your revisionist approach to history that doesn't demand suppositions based on fact." If I'd said that to him, I'm sure he would have thanked me for my support.

I could see, despite Tony's good nature that went along with his synaptic deprivations, that it was inevitable there would come a time when I could not sit still and watch him mangle our nation's history and our students' minds. That time came when he invited one of his "filler" speakers to class; someone from the John Birch Society. If you are not familiar with the John Birch society, it was a paranoid political group that began in the 1950s and held some notoriety during the 60s and 70s. The group saw communism growing at an alarming rate in the U.S. and found all sorts of secretive, communist plots to take over the government. In a nutshell, they were a group of crazy ultra-conservatives.

After the brainwashing that this speaker gave the students, they came to my class quivering in fear of hidden communist networks on the brink of destroying our country and the necessity of being vigilant in identifying these cells of evil. That had tipped the balance for me. I had neither the time nor the will to expend correcting all these misperceptions that had been foisted upon these naïve freshmen.

In anger, I went to the principal to plead my case. The only concession that I got was that I would be allowed to get another speaker to come to Mr. Ricci's class to provide an opposing point of view. When I explained my situation to a history professor at the nearby university, she volunteered to take up the cudgel of truth and do some damage control at our high school. Dr. Krueger gave them a wonderful lesson on the communist scare of the 50s with McCarthyism and the heroics of Edward R. Murrow. Also, she talked about the brand of anti-communism of the John Birchers and how uninformed and silly they were. Whew! Thank the gods they would be back to some sort of historical reality.

If you think that Ricci was upset, humiliated, or insulted by my intervention into his classroom affairs, then you have not yet assimilated the depth (or lack of depth) of this man's obliviousness. Tony was fine with everything that had occurred. He, even, thanked me for giving him another class period to study football plays (you didn't think he was going to hang around and listen to the speaker). I shook my head; it is hard to defeat such bliss.

*And yet...*despite his lack of academic worth, he had a following of boys that looked to him to initiate them into manhood. As a football coach, he inflicted the suffering and heroics necessary to make some young men civilized.

The teamwork and sacrifice necessary for football became their metaphor for cooperation in society. In my classes, I found that for certain students the only way I could motivate them to study was to tell them my grade could disqualify them from playing football. Often, that got the job done.

He had a following of young women as well. Of course, this was not to be unexpected from such a handsome man. But Ricci never flirted or was sexually inappropriate with these young women. He really did show them what male, adult behavior should be like toward teenage girls. He was happily married to a woman of equal beauty, who sometimes coached the cheerleaders. They were matched misfits of beauty like Ken and Barbie dolls, which is to say they were both attractive without a smattering of intellect. But they were the kind of couple that many of our students aspired to be, and they were more than willing to be sponsors for many dances and other social events.

Now for the salient question: should Tony Ricci, football coach extraordinaire and history teacher failure, be allowed to continue his work in secondary education? First of all, I think you are aware that Mr. Ricci would not be fired because of the importance of football in this high school. There were only two positions in this school district that required the approval of the school board: hiring a superintendent and hiring a football coach. That should give you an idea of the value placed on football in this school district.

What about never letting Tony into a history classroom again? Just give him sections of driver's training and P.E. For a number of reasons, this ideal schedule for Ricci was neither possible nor fair. There were too many coaches that wanted this kind of schedule, and they would turn on each other if any one of them were privileged.

This leaves us with a last solution that I would reluctantly support: give Coach Ricci his marching papers. Yes, it is valuable and important to initiate young men into manhood through football. I agree with Robert Bly – the lack of initiation ceremonies for young men is a problem in our society. Without these ceremonies, adolescent boys find other ways more dangerous and more criminal to prove their fearlessness and manhood. But, as I see it, we could have both with a new football coach that understands history. I would assume they're out there.

So sorry, Tony, but I'm sure you wouldn't understand.

Conclusion: They Smile When They Are Low

In writing about the misfits of the Jurassic, I am reminded that much of teachers' lives are like performers' lives. When you're in front of a class, students don't really care about your personal problems, your psychological needs, or your moods. No matter what, you have to be ready to put on the grease paint and go on with the show. The only place to hide – as I've written in Chapter 10 – is backstage in the faculty lounge. A teacher like an actor has to bring the energy to the audience, even if he or she doesn't feel like it, or else there won't be any reciprocal energy from the class.

The toll of this kind of investment of energy is what most people outside of the teaching profession overlook. They think it's fairly simple to relate information to students; students write it down, students are tested, and teachers do the grading. No big deal. But ask them how they feel when they have to do a simple hour presentation;

ask them about the tension they feel before, during, and after such a presentation. Usually, when they think of how difficult it would be to do this for an entire day to many unreceptive audiences, they begin to get an inkling of tensions in teaching. Walking a mile in a teacher's shoes is not far enough; we're talking marathons here. Summer is not just free time; it's time to heal.

I have fought the good fight with many wounded and heroic teachers. They have endured in crises while they put up a good front in order to carry out the difficult task of being stimulating for their students. I have been the misfit and the sad one on the faculty on occasion. During my divorce, I could barely get out of bed in the morning...*and yet*, with the support of my colleagues who had their own sorrows, I continued through the bleak days, which ended regularly with my collapsing in bed after school and trying to muster up enough energy so that I could return the next day.

I dedicate the following poem to all those denizens of blackboard and chalk, who overcame their personal grief and disappointment to appear each day at school with chipperness that belied the pall on their souls. I have been inspired by their courage and touched by their tragedies. I lock arms with them and march forward:

Blackboard and Chalk
I knew an abandoned teacher
who came home to a note on a table,
his marriage was on the rocks.
Yet he arrived the next morning,
blackboard and chalk,
and taught through the day in emotional shock.

And I knew a sexy teacher,
veiled in the failure of three marriages.
Students called her a fox.
Yet she arrived each morning,
blackboard and chalk,
and locked all her sorrows in a jewelry box.
And I knew the saddest of teachers
who swallowed his sorrows at supper
until he was as big as an ox.
Yet he was earliest to arrive in the morning,
blackboard and chalk,
every chink in his armor massively caulked.
And I knew an imprisoned teacher
who cared for a mother with memory loss.
Students mocked his penny loafers and white sox.
Yet he arrived every morning,
blackboard and chalk,
cheerful in his duties and all his bad luck.
And I knew an enchanted teacher
whose friends were dead poets.
A witch to the boys who were jocks.
Yet she appeared in the mornings,
blackboard and chalk,
casting spells in rhythms of Shakespeare and Frost.
And I knew a courageous teacher
without a shred of self-pity
who grew up in the school of hard knocks.
Yet with cancer he arrived in the mornings,
blackboard and chalk,
secretly dying as he stood like a rock.
And I've known teachers and teachers
of the tick and the tock

who metered their lives beneath classroom clocks.
Yet they arrived in all moods of the morning until
blackboard and chalk
dusted their hair white and withered their walks.
And I've known no complete erasure of teachers,
their talk and their talk,
that emanates still from building blocks.
The wax-coated corridors before students arrive
to blackboard and chalk
gleam with the dreams of all they have taught.

I love you all.

Chapter 12
Nobody Know the Changes I've Seen

"Our greatest intellectual adventures often occur within ourselves – not in the restless search for new facts and new objects on the earth or in the stars, but from a need to expunge old prejudices and build new conceptual structures. No hunt can promise a sweeter reward, a more admirable goal, than the excitement of thoroughly revised understanding...."

— Stephen Jay Gould

Each period in history is characterized by the special challenges that are salient at that point in time, whether it be war, plague, scientific discovery, etc. When I was growing up in the 50s, the challenge of the time was an understanding of the Cold War, Communism, and nuclear war. I remember going through school drills of what to do in case of nuclear war, drills that I must say wouldn't have helped save you in any way, except that you would have companionship before annihilation. I knew people that had nuclear bomb shelters, which all of us kids found to be a great place to play, drink, and look at *Playboy* magazines.

The challenge of the 60s, 70s, and 80s – the Jurassic – confronted the tumult of changing definitions and understandings of minorities. Questions about how much of a person's identity was the result of culture and how much was determined by biology dominated much of the discussion and changes that occurred during these years. Much of the Jurassic concerned itself with the new consciousness about minority issues and the implementation of this new, hard-fought-for awareness into the classrooms. Textbooks in English changed to include a new literary canon, vocabulary, and grammar. More inclusive American history textbooks were introduced, schools became more integrated, new courses were offered, and the faculty of schools became more mixed in ethnicity and gender.

I look back on these times, and I'm amazed at the changes that I've seen. But more than the changes that I've seen, I look back with a sense of accomplishment to the changes that occurred in me as a person. All of these issues of feminism, racism, and homosexuality had to be at first confronted by me as an individual before I could pass them on to students in the classroom. It was a matter of shucking off the assumptions that I was raised with: my father was a racist; my mother believed that a woman's role was to have babies, keep house, and stand by her man; and my parents were totally in the dark about how to detect or accommodate my gay brother.

In this chapter, I hope to give you a feel for the work of the Jurassic in terms of both the schools and my own wrestling with the issues. As Stephen Jay Gould states in the opening quote, it was the adventure of my times to reconceptualize, and nothing pleases me more than to think about how I opened up as a person and a teacher during the Jurassic.

He, She, It

When I was growing up in the 1950s, the roles of women and men were quite defined. Every woman in my neighborhood was a housewife and the bread baker. Their sense of competition had to do with who could get their clothes on the clothesline first. They all wore dresses and aprons; hats were a requirement to attend church on Sunday. All the men were expected to be the "bread" makers. They had their lunch pails in the morning and their jugs of beer in the evening. As far as I could tell, these gender roles were as fixed as male deer having antlers, while females did not.

When I went to school, there were few roles for girls in sports, which seemed reasonable to me considering their future roles in society. I remember the first time in high school I saw a girl with serious muscles. She was a swimmer for the local swim club and a contender for a spot in the Olympics. I felt sorry for her – how was she ever going to get a man with muscles like that!

Without belaboring the point, I was culturally hypnotized into what was masculine and what was feminine. Then came the birth of Women's Lib in the late 60s. At about the same time as men were burning their draft cards, women were reputed to be burning their bras (we know today that this was a myth created by the media). Along with reading about protests by feminists, I began reading some of the seminal literature of the second wave movement – *The Feminine Mystique* by Betty Friedan and *Sexual Politics* by Kate Millett. This was the beginning of intellectual doubt for me, which led to some epistemological thinking as I traced the origins of masculine and feminine and the reality of the patriarchy.

On the personal level, many of the women I knew and dated claimed to be feminists, and they began forcefully yet patiently opening my eyes to what it was like to be "imprisoned" in the female body. By the time I got into the classroom, I was convinced of the rightness of the feminist cause, even though I had much to learn and relearn. Soon, I noticed my textbooks began to include more literature by and about women, with "Story of an Hour" by Kate Chopin being one of my favorites.

There were vocabulary changes that came about because of the second wave, and they came crashing into the classroom. "What's this Ms. thing and how is it pronounced?" "Why should we say humanity rather than mankind?" "Is there really any difference between *policeman* and *police officer*?" I never approached the answers to these questions with the fervor of a missionary seeking converts. These terms and titles were just beginning to seep into culture, and they were far from being totally accepted. All I tried to do was to help my classes understand the debate. If I could get as far as that, I found my efforts to be a victory.

Vocabulary changes, while relevant, are the easiest changes to make when you come on board or are forced to come on board the ship of change. With feminism, it was fairly simple to incorporate new terms; for instance, use *Ms.*, use *women* instead of *girls* for females over 16, and avoid *gals*. But feminism, unlike any of the other minority movements, went much deeper into the language with a change in pronoun usage. We use pronouns far more than any other words in our vocabularies. If we are going to make changes in their usage, we are talking about far more effort than substituting one term for another or extinguishing some terms.

The problem of integrating feminism into English has to do with an anomaly embedded into English – the third person singular pronouns (*he, she, it*) have gender. *I, you* (singular and plural), *we, they* are gender-neutral, which means it doesn't matter whether their antecedents are male or female. Before feminism, if we didn't know the gender of a third person singular, the default pronoun was the masculine. With feminism, we were confronted with a whole new frontier of pronoun problems. This is where the sentence "If a student wants to go to college, *he* must take the ACT" requires a new focus. Should we write, "he or she must, ""he/she must," "she/he must" or change "a student" to "students" and then use "they"?

These and more pronoun changes came into the classroom before they were incorporated into college entrance exams – the ACT and the SAT – which caused me to be teaching two systems of grammar side by side. The same was true with various business organizations: some accepted the new feminist grammar; others retained the status quo grammar. On the whole, businesses were conservative in the use of feminist terms and grammar. *The NY Times*, for instance, waited until 1986 before embracing *Ms.* So, I told my students that in the environment of their times, they needed to ask their employers what their grammar preferences were.

With feminism, teaching grammar in high school during the Jurassic was an activity fraught with debate and emotion. But it was exciting, and I wouldn't change these difficulties for a well-diagrammed sentence.

Apocalypse IX

I remember the end of the world coming on June 23, 1972. The world ends quite often in history, and I had seen it end previously on July 2, 1964, when the Civil Rights Law came into effect. Apocalypse IX would come when President Nixon signed into law an educational amendment that prohibited sexual discrimination in any federally funded schools. A cry went out from high school coaches, athletic directors, and administrators that Title IX would be the end of sports programs for males.

As an English teacher and occasional coach of minor sports, I had little opinion on what this might mean for the future of male sports. All I knew was that as the years passed by, I observed more and more sports programs available for young women and more and more young women participating in these sports. And here is where I learned something about masculine and feminine on the gut level, the most profound and long-lasting way to learn.

Sad to say that while intellectually I understood the linguistics of feminism, I did not understand what physical potential and aggressive behavior was locked inside the female body. In the beginning of the implementation of Title IX, I began attending some of the girls' volleyball and basketball games, and I was shocked that these girls were the same "feminine" creatures that I taught in my classes. There was no daintiness about them. They had athleticism, competitive emotion, team spirit, and toughness. They took their sports seriously, and sometimes they were even downright vicious. *Sally Brinkman, vicious? Why she's one of the sweetest people I've ever met.* Yet, there she was crashing the boards for a rebound and elbowing everybody in sight.

It was time for a revamping of what I thought about female bodies and psychologies. It was apparent that sports and physical activity were just as important to women as they were to men. They needed the outlet just as much – maybe more with all the restrictions they had grown up with about being "a lady." And, it didn't change them into men. They were just as capable of dressing up in gowns for the prom as were the football players dressing up in suits and ties. But I did notice that the adolescent girls that participated in sports seemed to be more comfortable in their bodies and less inclined to depend on adolescent boys for an identity.

As it goes with all turnings of history's odometer to zeroes, there are groups that predict the coming of the apocalypse. The day after the turn of the century from 1899 to 1900, the headline in the *NY Times* read "World Fails to End." I would like to say the same about the coming of Title IX – "Men's Sports Fail to End." All the fears and dire predictions of women being included in sports programs were much ado about nothing. Since 1972, sports programs of both men and women have continued to grow and thrive. To see women in sports roles and even in the armed forces has become normalized.

But I remember when it wasn't in the Jurassic. And I remember how glad I was that my daughter, a millennial, did not have to cope with these physical limitations, and how we played sports together and how I coached some of her girl teams. I always told people, "She's the son I always wanted."

(As a final note, I would like to say that my gender concepts did not only change with women but, also, with men. As a man, I was handed a lot of fairy tales about what it was to be a man. Many of the male roles that I witnessed around me didn't excite me very much. The following is a poem I wrote about the male quandary and disappointments.)

From Brothers Grimm
they told us fairy tales for men
we would be giants growing into clouds
frogs that kissed like princes
Jacks with magic sticks
we'd get the girl in the forest
covered in glass
a pastry with cherry lips
only we must work to be worthy
whistle in drudgery of tunnels
gather gold from a coarse ore
the woman of the forest
would be waiting at day's end
a princess to fill our pails
but the princess came with
stained apron and rough hands
wisps of hair clinging to a sweaty face
and she swelled like an apple
each child another bite from a lean budget
with graying temples
we asked the mirror one day
"who are we?"

the mirror replied
"you are the dwarves"

ours was to work metals of darker regions,
to bald with potbellies
stare into mugs of beer
ours to come home late
to find the women we loved
pretending to be asleep
later years find us
naked before the mirror
not recognizing ourselves
yellowed memories flicker in the glass
urging us to rise
to dance in iron slippers
but we are wheeled entranced
to the nodding room
where old men descend
below flowers never
to be awakened ever after

You've Got To Be Carefully Taught

Just as in the song from the musical *South Pacific*, I was carefully taught as a child to be prejudiced. It was apparent to me that blacks were inferior to whites. When we drove by the projects in my city, it was easy to see black people didn't take care of their property or their clothes, that they drank alcohol on their stoops, and that their behavior was not subdued like "civilized" people. I didn't have a historical perspective as a child, and this is the kind of thinking (or lack of thinking) upon which self-fulfilling prophecies depend.

I witnessed more racism in my family's restaurant, not in the deep South, but in central Illinois. We did not serve blacks. If you had the audacity as a black person to sit at one of our tables, that's all you would do – sit, because no one was going to serve you. We did, however, allow Negroes (the correct term of the time) to order food to go.

During the 60s with its civil rights turmoil, my carefully taught prejudices were brought to a crisis. My ignorance (and that is what it was) could no longer be supported by the facts. I was fortunate that my first history teacher in high school was, also, the first black man in our local educational system. He was not shy about laying out the facts as history unfolded before our very eyes on television – Martin Luther King, Malcolm X, Selma, the Black Panthers, etc. And I changed.

After all the tumult and shouting between my father and me and my father's hysteria about how our restaurant would be going hell in a handbasket if our restaurant served black people, our restaurant was forced to change. What amazed me was that after about a month of black customers coming to our restaurant just to convince themselves that they could, it was over. Just 30 days! Soon our restaurant had our black regulars, and we were the better for it both financially and socially. Another "World Fails to End" scenario.

A New Soliloquy

Just as with feminism, I was in lockstep with the acceptable vocabulary moving from *Colored People, Negro, Black, Afro-American* to *African American*. Discussions about proper terminology were a part of my English classes, and the inevitable debates about Mark Twain's use of "nigger" and the use of "nigger" within the black community itself resulted. All provided enlightening, energetic, and questing material in integrated classrooms.

Then, came the Ebonics issue. Was black English a language in its own right or a dialect of Standard English? Should it be taught in the high schools and accepted in writing assignments? One of my favorite responses to this was to have my students rewrite Hamlet's soliloquy in Ebonics. It proved to be an interesting comparison because Shakespearean English was as remote to many of my students as was Black English (not all of my black students were that familiar with Ebonics either). Both required a ton of annotations in order for some readers to make heads or tails out of Hamlet's speech. Here's an example of the exercise that I wrote years later when the internet was available:

Ham[1] Speakin' It

I be, or not be – you know what I'm sayin':
Whether it ain't no thang bruthaz be messed wit
An' catch a F[2],
Or we be takin' no shih
An' bust a cap[3] in some whitey jake[4].
To die, get high –
No mo – an' wif a deuce[5] or dime's worth[6], BAYAM[7],
We be ending dis pain shih
An' it all be good in dis hoodt,
Daswhat flesh wit heroin do. It be fly[8]
Totally to be wasted. To die, get high –
Get high – purchase sum ice[9]: dang, dere's da tweek[10],
For in dat sleep of meth you be crashin' and freakin'

When u be snufflin' off dis metal foil,
You know dat. Dere's disrespect
Dat makes fo so short life.
Check it, foo,
For who wanna be whipped[11] an' pimped an' shih,
Wit wankstas[12] drysnitchin'[13] an' dissin', talkin' smack, or
Sum skeeza[14] burn u wit da germ[15], Popo[16] smokin' yo
sherm[17],
Peeps[18] be getting' in yo bidness, and jockin' yo style[19],
When u could be chillin' wif some blow[20] in yo' crib
Wida bare-ass beyotch? Who would fo-fo's[21] bear,
Representin'[22] in dis janky[23] life,
But somethin' wit swagga[24] befo death,
Ballin'[25] in dese projects where u be born,
An' no whitey traveler returns, muzzles da will,
An' make us bear dese ills we have
than flip da script[26] to others dat we doan know of?
Thus thuggin'[27] do make gangstas[28] of us all,
An' thus we excuse our native hues
An' blame dose wit a pale cast of skin.
An' black activists of great pitch and protest
we disregard to act da foo[29]
An' abuse da name of affirmative action. – Yo,
Serious[30] sistah Oprah! – u be speakin' HO-rizons,
But daswhatsup.

Annotations

1. Crazy – used in Southern ebonics
2. According to Big L's song "Ebonics," "If you caught a felony, you caught a F"
3. shoot
4. *MrWiggles' Ghetto Glossary* – cop

5. *Drug Slang Dictionary* – amount of heroin to cause death
6. *Drug Slang Dictionary* – heroin; $2 worth of drugs
7. *DA GANGSTA PAGE* – means to hit or strike
8. cool in style
9. *Urban Dictionary* – crystallized meth
10. *Urban Dictionary* – the nervous ticks or twitching one experiences as they come down from a crystal methamphetamine binge
11. *Urban Dictionary* – when a man is controlled by his girlfriend to the point of embarrassment to his friends
12. *Urban Dictionary* – people who wanna be ganstas
13. *MSN Encarta Dictionary* – the act of informing on somebody indirectly either by talking loudly or by acting suspiciously in the presence of police officers or prison guards
14. *Urban Dictionary* – prostitute
15. From Big L's song "Ebonics" – "burn u wit da germ" means gives you AIDS
16. *Bay Area from Vox Communications* – police
17. According to Big L's song "Ebonics," "Angel dust is sherm"
18. people
19. *Dictionary of Black Slang* – copycatting you
20. cocaine
21. *Bay Area from Vox Communications* – forty-four caliber pistols
22. *MrWiggles' Ghetto Glossary* – go all out for yourself or crew, or anything you're down with or stand for

23. *Bay Area from Vox Communications* – something that is bad or lousy
24. *Urban Dictionary* – one's own unique style or personality that sets you apart from anyone else
25. *Urban Dictionary* – living a life of extreme wealth and flaunting it
26. *Bay Area from Vox Communications* – to lie or change your story
27. *Urban Dictionary* – doing whatever it takes to survive...selling drugs, robbing, rapping or Day-to-Day hustling
28. *Urban Dictionary* – someone who lives in the projects and is usually in a gang
29. *Bay Area from Vox Communications* – to act up, to do something stupid, or to get in trouble
30. *Ebonics-Translator* – that which is extreme in its tenacity

The assignment was a little risky, but I found students learned a lot about linguistics and they participated like dogs on the hunt either volunteering knowledge about Ebonics or seeking Ebonics' sources. As they progressed through Shakespeare's soliloquy and translated it to Ebonics, they learned *Hamlet*, appreciated Hamlet's speech all the more, and they became more aware of how language evolves and how what was standard English at one time may succumb to a variety of changes.

The Zulus Are Coming

I cannot leave this subject of race issues in high school without mentioning one endearing story about an all-white, rural high school in Illinois where I taught. This school district was segregated as a matter of geography and occupation. It was too far out for any bussing program to integrate the school, and the surrounding area was mainly farmland with no black farmers.

However, as the suburbs of the nearest big city expanded, one suburb of metropolitan area encroached on this school district's boundaries. And in this suburb, there happened to be just one black family. This family that had recently moved in was going to have to send their two daughters of high school age to an all-white rural school. I'm sure the parents recalled scenes of Ruby Bridges flanked by federal marshals.

But these parents were quite special. First of all, they were tall, slender people who carried themselves with the pride of Zulu warriors. They dressed well and had about them an expressionless gaze that could not be demeaned. They stood out in all the events at school as they looked over us all like members of a Greek chorus. They never said much or mixed much, but they never appeared shy or uncomfortable.

The girls had picked up this same kind of self-assuredness. There was an aura around Vanessa and Tamara that brooked no tolerance for any kind of racial comments. And I never saw one confrontation during their years at our school because I believe no one ever wanted to tangle with the Mowry sisters.

But what was wonderful about all this was that the Mowry sisters slid into a comfortable existence at our school without a blip of trouble. I was amazed at how quickly they became integrated into a white, working-class school. They were wonderful, and soon it was clear that it would be hard to imagine the school without having them around.

They stole the teachers' hearts by being hardworking and straight-A students. Socially, other students liked them, and they participated in many activities in the school – yearbook, student government, float building, plays, etc. Vanessa, the taller of the sisters, gave the community something to cheer about when she spiked a volleyball down the throats of our opposition. She went on to college with a volleyball scholarship. Yes, it was apparent to all in the school the goodness and worth of these two girls. But what was really the coup de grace for me and what made me silent on a peak in Darien was that Vanessa was voted homecoming queen.

Sometimes in the midst of the fight against prejudice, we (yes, I, a white man, consider myself as part of the fight) throw up our hands in despair at the entrenched hatred and smallness of some people. But once in a while, we see an act of hope to reinforce the belief of a basic goodness in humankind. I loved the lack of self-consciousness about Vanessa becoming homecoming queen in an all-white school. In the students' minds, she was beautiful, talented, smart, and affable and, therefore, deserved to be homecoming queen. There was nothing black and white about it, except her qualifications. This kind of colorless decision is the vision that we seek for the eventual demise of racism. This school showed me that what must be done, can be done. I do not despair.

Enola Gays

In the area of sexuality, there were two bombshells in my life with magnitudes of Hiroshima and Nagasaki. The first was delivered by my youngest brother, who revealed to me when I had just gone to college that he was a homosexual. At the time I wish he had told me that he was secretly a Martian because then I could have had him committed with no sense of guilt. In 1966, the year of this confession, I had only heard it rumored that there were people who perversely had same-gender sex. One must remember there was no mention of homosexuality in movies, on TV, and in my reading. From the little I knew I thought these homosexuals were definitely perverse, mentally ill, and deserved criminal punishment.

But it's easy to have definite opinions about subjects that don't affect you personally. I loved my brother and his revelation was a wrench in the works. What to do? What advice to give? I hadn't a clue. It was a secret between him and me; the other family members weren't aware. Since I was in college, I decided to take some psychology and sociology courses to see if they had some answers to a host of questions that I had about homosexuality. Then there was the theological side of it. As a Catholic, I began to look at the moral-religious side of homosexuality and the pertinent biblical passages.

But more educational than anything academic, I began meeting gay people. When my brother went to college near St. Louis, during my visits I accompanied him as he moved around the gay nightlife of the city. I met with and stayed with his gay friends. After graduating from college and being drafted into the army, my journey into understanding and meeting homosexuals continued. There were many gays in the army that preferred to go to Vietnam rather than apply for a Section 8. I found it amazing that their fear of being "outed" by the army trumped their fear of going to Vietnam. Thus, by the time I began to teach in the early 70s, I had learned a lot about homosexuality and had strong opinions about what it meant to be gay.

The second bombshell was delivered in 1973 – the American Psychiatric Association removed homosexuality from its handbook of mental disorders. It confirmed the strong opinions that I had already from my encounters with so many gays – that is, homosexuality was neither a perversion nor a crime. The implication of the American Psychiatric Association's decision was a nuclear explosion: could it be that being gay was NORMAL! Even more than Stonewall, this conclusion was a blow to any reasoned arguments against homosexuality. It had scientific backing, and the evidence was compelling.

Now came the huge question: what to do about this as a teacher? By comparison, racism and feminism were simple matters to introduce into the classroom, but homosexuality ran much deeper with taboos, religious condemnation, and a yawning pit of ignorance. Such societal traditions lead to some very intense conscious and unconscious fears. As Yoda would say in *Star Wars* (I hope his authority provides a little levity with truth), "Fear leads to anger...anger leads to hate...hate leads to suffering."

I had listened to the suffering stories of so many gays – the suicide attempts, the self-loathing, the drugs and alcohol, the rejections by family, religion and society – that I could not apply to this minority the former use of the word *gay*. To live a secretive life, to be despised by society because of something you could not help, and to repress all your sexual feelings is a formula for anxiety and depression.

I knew there was no way that I could tackle gay rights head-on in the classroom without packing my bags and heading off to another profession. However, it pained me to think that so many of my students were gay (consciously or unconsciously) without a clue or a model from the mainstream to guide them through their existential crises.

So, as I mentioned in my chapter "Teacher as Subversive," I casually made mention of the fact that many of the authors that we studied were gay. It was a small seed planted, to be sure, but it proclaimed, "Fear not young man or woman if you are gay or lesbian. There are others like you, and they have made great contributions to the world." I, also, made mention that I had a gay brother that lived in San Francisco, where there were so many gays that they had their own neighborhoods. This appalled straight students (and I let them have their say; this was not a conversion session), but it whispered to those that were gay, "And if you endure young gay man or woman, you can leave your locality and make a pilgrimage to a mecca meant just for you." Finally, I liked to hand out the delightful Heterosexual Questionnaire designed by Martin Rochlin, Ph.D., in 1972. Its introduction started with these words:

"This questionnaire is for self-avowed heterosexuals only. If you are not openly heterosexual, pass it on to a friend who is. Please try to answer the questions as candidly as possible. Your responses will be held in strict confidence and your anonymity fully protected."

Amazingly, in a short period of time, we have gotten past such things. We now have openly gay TV shows, movies, and politicians. There are gay organizations right in the high schools. Gay literature has come so far that now we not only read gay literary works in class, but we have a form of literary criticism called "Queer Theory." The last bombshell came when the Supreme Court made gay marriage legal. Yet it pains me to see there are still a few state holdouts. These states have what is called "no promo homo" laws, which forbids positively portraying homosexuality in any way. This is a last dying gasp because the genie has been released from the bottle, and no matter what these schools do, their homosexual students will have the exposure that is required to not only endure but to prevail (thanks, William Faulkner for the phrase).

When the AIDS epidemic began in the 80s, I was appalled by the lack of compassion for the gay community in the beginning. I was kept apprised of the situation by my brother in San Francisco and, of course, I was immensely worried about his contracting the virus. It got so bad in San Francisco as time went on that my brother took a year sabbatical from his job to help friends die and then to spread their ashes. When he told me about a dinner party he went to where everyone at the table had been given the death sentence with an HIV-positive diagnosis, it was an image that percolated in my mind until it came out as a poem. As you will notice in this poem, I turned this dinner party into a kind of biblical Last Supper scene told from the only survivor, who is a kind of Peter/John figure. The poem is dedicated to the first gay person that I knew personally that died of AIDS.

Fading Photograph of the Last Supper
for Curt Pilatz (1948-88)

in memory of you

I do

drinking a glass of wine
I hold an old photograph
and remember your revelation

with head on shoulder
you whispered in my ear
all here were infected with mystery

save me

death a palpable presence
Phillip's ebullience, denial
Thomas's eyes distant on doubtful years
Jude's active fingers belying calm on his face
James drawing cigarettes with seething anger

all betrayed

"It's in my body. It's in my blood.
Let this virus pass from me."
I drank until I could barely stand

we drove to the park above the city
I sobered in night air
lights streamed in arteries below
I held your hand
while you recited final things

you'd return

home to the father
tell him you were gay
tell him you had AIDS
that you loved him
that you forgave him
that he could be redeemed

before I could comfort you
flashlights scorched our faces
cops had us step out of the car
I swung at one and caught him in the ear
that's when you stepped in front
to take the crushing blow meant

for me

I awoke alone in a cell
calling your name
my shirt and pants blood splattered
no one answered
charges were dropped when I denied

witnessing

I ran to your home
where everyone gathered
they told me you were dead
a single sentence in the papers
to record your passing

by miracle I am the only one
left in this fading photograph

Jude committed suicide
James's and Andrew's ashes remain on my mantel
the rest abandoned to the dead to bury

the dead

the old places hold no ghosts
a generation martyred
a world without our past
sometimes I begin to doubt
you existed at all

only when I sleep
do you come to me across the waters
revived in those weekends on our boat
when you'd bend the mast to fill the sails
and together in spray

we'd ascend

Conclusion:

I have seen a lot of changes during my time and during the Jurassic. Each generation is entrusted with a sacred duty to carry on the good work of the past and to engage the new dangers of their own times. In my day, we fought for a new consciousness about men and women, gay and straight, and white and black.

This quest fits in well with American history and style – to erase the boundaries between people and to humanize minorities. From the beginning, our nation was the experiment for the erasure of religious differences, class differences, and national origins. Then we moved to the profound encounters with slavery and voting rights for women. The quest never stops and the accomplishments of the 60s are not an end but just a mileage marker as we as a society continue the marathon work of our ancestors. You'd think we'd be used to it by now.

I realize that many of the subjects that I've discussed are extremely sensitive in today's climate, even though one might have thought that we had gone beyond some. The scope of gender and feminism is larger than before. The Me Too movement has opened up hushed stories of the abuses of women in the workplace. LGBTQ has replaced LGBT (the abbreviation continues to grow in some circles with LGBTQIA) with transgender rights and the breaking down of the confines of approaching gender in binary terms. Further, it's once more to the breach with racism and the Black Lives Matter movement.

I hope I have approached these subjects with as much care and sensitivity as possible. If I have offended, I plead ignorance but with a willingness in my clumsiness to learn and change. As I stated in the introduction of this chapter, the most rewarding changes are those that occur inside. Overcoming locked-in perceptions so as to see things in a new light is the noble path. This re-seeing life and re-visioning the future is as exciting as it gets. Let us hope we never get rid of the idea of Utopia or the hope that humanity can be improved.

Chapter 13
Notes from Pisgah

After retiring from teaching and having the time and height to view my past, I conclude we've been very tentative in our approaches to education. My nostalgia for the good old days does not outweigh the gnawing thought – I could have done so much more, and the system could have done so much more.

The configurations of the classroom, the high school buildings (with the abomination of trailers), the curricula, the administrators, etc. haven't changed as much as they should have since the Jurassic. I know that it wouldn't take me long to be up to speed in current high schools because I have made many presentations at many different high schools in the last couple of years, and I always leave feeling that I could begin where I left off. The question is would I like to begin where I left off? I would have to answer with an emphatic NO.

With all the new equipment and advances in knowledge and with all the new openness that we tout, I expect much more from the present educational system. Sometimes, I have found that not only has education been stifled, but it has actually regressed. One biology teacher for advanced students, for example, told me recently that 80% of her class is about knowing the definitions of terms so that her students do well on THE TEST. Really! Are we preparing students to go on *Jeopardy*? Then, I thought about my high school biology teacher, who, when one of us hit a fox with his truck on the way to school, thought nothing of bringing it to class. Mr. Shane immediately put aside the day's lesson plans, had us roll up our sleeves so that we could dissect it. A little more ghoulish than memorizing terms. A helluva of a lot more informative. A helluva lot more like biology.

In this chapter, I want to share with you my Moses experiences from Pisgah and the visions I had for a promised land that was not to be. But maybe as compensation for my loss in such aridity, I will get to live to be a hundred and twenty like Moses.

The Play's the Thing

I got my first glimpse of how learning could be configured differently when I was hired at a new school and, of course, got assigned a new duty that others in the department did not want. I would be responsible for the senior play. It made no difference to the superintendent or principal that I had never been in a play, let alone directed one. The only extracurricular duty that required experience in this school system was the football coach. Otherwise, any-*body* would do.

Begrudgingly, I began reading up on play craft and checking out our stage facilities, which were few.

Apparently, drama equipment was not as high on the list of purchases as football equipment. Thankfully, the play was not scheduled until spring of the second semester, and I would have time to gather resources, to learn some skills, and to recruit some actors.

Since I was not the senior college-bound English teacher, the pool of actors I would recruit from would mainly be my "sweathog" senior English classes. I use the term "sweathogs" affectionately as did Gabe Kaplan in the popular TV series at the time called *Welcome Back, Kotter.* These students were not as homogeneous as the college-bound English classes. They comprised an odd mixture of students who were smart enough to be in advanced classes, but were not ambitious; students that had a lot of mechanical skills whether with cars and motorcycles or stereo equipment; some that came across and dressed as if they were tough and wild, but in essence that was a façade for many vulnerabilities; others had dreams that had nothing to do with college – being rock stars, members of the armed services, hairstylists, etc. And, yes, some were just dimwitted, like Vinnie Barbarino on *Welcome Back, Kotter.*

Naturally, I wanted to pick a play that I thought they could handle – something simple and lighthearted. I decided to go with a melodrama called *Love Rides the Rails (or Will the Mail Train Run Tonight?).* I purchased enough copies so that I could begin the New Year by doing the first read-through in my classes.

The project quickly picked up momentum. The casting was almost done by the class itself. Almost everyone knew who the villainous Simon Darkway should be, the helpless maiden Carlotta Cortez, the idiot assistant to the villain

Dirk Sneath, etc. Volunteers were plentiful and eager to do the sound system and to gather the equipment. Sources for lumber, tools, and canvas to make sets appeared out of nowhere (I didn't question anyone how or where they had come by some of these materials).

Then Randy, a rock band lead guitarist, proposed the "ridiculous" idea that we could make this play into a musical. ("Oh, god, no," I said to myself. I was in over my head already.) A number of my pupils played musical instruments (mainly rock and country band instruments) and a few of them had really good voices. Reluctantly, I told the classes that I would take the idea to the band instructor, since I had little knowledge about musical scores and coordinating songs and drama. Did I say, "little knowledge"? How about no knowledge.

Ms. Beth Merriman was just out of college and saddled with her first job as band instructor. To say she was overwhelmed with her new responsibilities would be an understatement. Yet, as much as I gave her every opportunity to say no, she loved musicals and wanted to be a part of our production. What was even more intriguing, Beth had been a dancer and knew how to choreograph.

Soon everyone got caught up in the new enterprise. With few complaints, we spent evenings and weekends building sets, making costumes, setting up lighting and sound systems. People were learning skills in all sorts of areas. I found it amazing how many kids I had to teach how to use a hammer and saw. Personally, I learned to use a sewing machine. By the time we had reached the moment of the opening performance, I believe Ms. Merriman and I earned about 25 cents an hour for the time we had put in. But all of us knew we had put together something special.

Indeed, the show was a smashing success. But what influenced me the most was the afterglow of accomplishment. All those who had participated in this simple drama had overcome obstacles, solved problems, and learned new skills. They were full of themselves, and I accredited this to the fact that they felt *competent*. For many in the play, school was never a place where they could show any kind of competency. School aggravated their shortcomings by isolating them in competitive settings of learning. I didn't *teach* math when we were building sets, but they *did* math all the time calculating materials for sets and stage size. I didn't *teach* research, but placement of lights and sound systems required looking up the best configurations. The list goes on of what all of us had learned – choreography, music, the history of melodrama, electrical systems, building and painting skills, etc.

"Could," I asked, myself, "this collective enterprise be a way to configure education in the future?" Maybe the departmentalization and compartmentalization of high school was too narrow of a system to disperse knowledge. Maybe we needed something more inclusive of fields of study and projects more collaborative and egalitarian among teachers, students, and community. Like for Hamlet, the play was the thing that started me on the road of conceiving new kinds of schools and classes.

In Search of a Unified Field Theory of Education

Once I had determined the effectiveness of learning experiences with larger scopes, I began a more conscious search for people and models of inspiration. In many ways, as I approached the 21st century, I felt like Henry Adams in *The Education of Henry Adams* as he approached the 20th century. Adams felt in his later years that much of what he had learned in school was inadequate for dealing with the changing times. I began wondering if what I was teaching was more useful to times past. Thus, I started to collect the bits and pieces of my intellectual life that could, perhaps, give me some themes I could use if I were to invent new classes and new ways of organizing those classes (it should be pointed out that this search came before the electronic revolution of computers and cell phones).

Pisgah in Black Mountain

One of the most impressive experiments in education was the establishment of Black Mountain College in Black Mountain, North Carolina. This innovative college was short-lived and only existed between the years of 1933 and 1957. I became aware of Black Mountain College because whenever I researched the biographies of the people who were influential to my artistic and intellectual growth, I found that many of them had either been faculty or graduates of this little-known college in the Blue Ridge Mountains (and near, by the way, to the American Mt. Pisgah).

Robert Creeley and the Black Mountain poets put their stamp on my interest in poetry and in writing poetry. Buckminster Fuller and Kenneth Snelson nursed my love for architecture and sculpture. In the areas of painting and assemblage art, I was inspired by Cy Twombly and Robert

Rauschenberg. Then there was John Cage and the "Happening." The list goes on.

How did an educational institution that lasted only twenty-three years and had fewer than 1,200 graduates assemble and produce so many great people? It certainly had nothing to do with money because Black Mountain College operated on a shoestring budget. Foremost, I would say they were imbued with John Dewey's educational philosophy:

"...compartmentalization of occupations and interests bring about a separation of that mode of activity commonly called 'practice' from insight, of imagination from executive 'doing.' Each of these activities is then assigned its own place which it must abide. Those who write the anatomy of experience then suppose that these divisions in here in the very constitution of human nature." — John Dewey

In accordance with Dewey's principles of education, Black Mountain College had all their students labor in all aspects of the school from growing food to building a new school at a second location. They definitely believed in hands-on. Secondly, the lines between subjects were either blurred or disposed of. There was no C. P. Snow's division of the humanities and sciences. Dance, physics, architecture, poetry, etc. were all blended into makeshift classes that had no prescribed time frames, except lunch and supper. There were lots of evenings of lectures, plays, and dance performances by students, faculty, and guests. Finally, there was a driving democratic spirit with no hierarchical distinctions between students and faculty –

everyone was there to learn from each other; school rules, classes, and policies were made collectively by everyone in the school.

Ironically enough, in this experimental school, Buckminster Fuller (an architect), Merce Cunningham (a dancer), and John Cage (a composer) met every morning for breakfast and began working out another experimental school that would caravan from city to city. There was no shortage of creativity at Black Mountain College.

Undoubtedly, this college was a special educational *institution* (if so restricted a word could be used) with results that resonated through the cultural scene of the last half of the twentieth century. From this experiment, I learned what could happen when you open up the educational process and provide students with more holistic experiences.

People Come and Go Talking of Henry David Thoreau

Black Mountain was a fascinating experiment, but the really great experiment in education was the founding of our nation. The quality of education that emerges at this time was called by other nations "Yankee Ingenuity." What was it that made Yankee ingenuity possible and why have we lost it today?

The weight of the old European cultures did not hold down the inventive, the entrepreneurial, and the egalitarian of the New World. Three examples of this spirit came to mind as I was thinking about transforming our present educational system: Benjamin Franklin, Thomas Jefferson, and Henry David Thoreau. What was it about these men that attracted me both as an American and as an educator?

First of all, they all had that pragmatism of the New World, that can-do spirit. There was no technology Franklin touched that he couldn't improve, whether it be the traditional fireplace, stoves, lamplights, or the delivery of the mail. Jefferson, as well, was constantly tinkering with everything from building a sinuous wall one-brick thick to the mortarboard plow. Then, there's Thoreau, who was responsible for a host of inventions. Thoreau's family made pencils and, when he worked for his father after college, he invented a machine to better refine graphite, which resulted in Thoreau Pencils becoming the most sought-after pencils in the U.S. Besides my interest in Franklin's, Jefferson's, and Thoreau's inventive genius, I was completely bowled over by the fact that none of these three men were interested in making money from their inventions. They all left their inventions unpatented to be shared by the general public. Entrepreneurs, but not **greedy** entrepreneurs.

What catches me off guard about the "Big Three" is that their genius was not relegated to one area. These American men, nourished in American soil, were not restrained like their European counterparts. Birthrights, class ceilings, religious/philosophical boundaries, and curriculum restrictions in learning didn't put up roadblocks to their pursuits. Thus, we have an architect, inventor, lawyer, entrepreneur like Jefferson write the *Declaration of Independence*. We have the surveyor, Harvard educated, hut builder, inventor, essayist like Thoreau write "Civil Disobedience" and influence Gandhi and Martin Luther King in the succeeding century. Finally, we have Franklin, humorist, printer, and on the cutting edge of science and the hanging edge of politics.

These "Yanks" and their uniquely American approach to learning is what I would want in my future vision for contemporary education. To me, the U.S. has gone the way of all revolutions – the fresh spirit of a beginning gives way to the solidifying of new gains that gives way to the overweight sluggishness of sitting on past laurels. Our educational system had reached the last stage of this process: the anti-establishment becomes the stodgy establishment. There is a need for a new infusion of ideas.

The Top Ten

Besides Black Mountain College and "the Big Three," I collected a lot of examples in search of a new unified field theory of education. From Bucky Fuller's World Game, I learned how to think globally and how to think about using mainframe computers to collect and analyze data to save the world from itself. As I dug deeper into art and science, despite C.P. Snow's "The Two Cultures," I found the untold story about artists and scientists is that they worked well together. Reimagining space and time were a pre-occupation of both artists and scientists in the 20th century, and they often played off one another. The collaborations between Billy Klüver, the bohemian engineer of Bell Laboratories, and the Greenwich Village artists in the 50s through 70s is a parable of what can be done when different "fields" reach across artificial fences.

The resources I found were abundant – too many to categorize here – but there were a few themes that I will list here in my re-visioning the educational system of the Jurassic:

1. build or make something
2. make sure everyone learns vocational skills
3. fuse and interconnect many subject areas
4. open up the physical space of classrooms and schools
5. travel to learn
6. no grades and no bells
7. consider art as central and not ancillary
8. use local volunteers and expertise
9. use teachers collaboratively from as many disciplines as possible
10. take risks while obviating litigation

These ten criteria are what I used in my first attempts of thinking up new classes during my tenure as a secondary teacher. It will be no surprise that they were never tried, but I hope that you will see some merit in the two examples below.

Return to Huckleberry

I was born on the Mississippi River in Quincy, Illinois, just 15 miles from Hannibal, Missouri. Therefore, I was steeped in the mythologies of Mark Twain, Tom Sawyer, and Huckleberry Finn. As a child, I roamed free; my parents seldom knew where I was. They would have been shocked by how often I played with friends by the river trying to build a raft and float down the Mississippi to have adventures. We never got far enough to actually launch a raft, having few skills and fewer tools, but we gave each attempt our all no matter the sweltering, summer days, the blisters, and the mosquito bites.

From this was born my first visionary educational activity for boys at risk. I will say right at the outset that it was an outrageous idea and probably just as unlikely to launch as my childhood raft, but I believed it would work, even though I could never get anyone to buy into it.

My empathy has always gone out to the Huckleberry Finn, delinquent boy. I grew up with many in this fold that I split ways within high school as they pursued lives of bad boys, and I became a compliant child of the system. But I was convinced this didn't have to be if the educational system could reach them at this critical time between middle school and high school.

"Return to Huckleberry" was my name for a program, where boys would build a raft under the tutelage of many in the community – teachers of many subjects, local carpenters and craftsmen, entertainers, fishermen, and more. An entire school year would be devoted to these boys where they would have a schedule that included:

- raft building: construction people in the area would help them design and put together rafts that would hold three to five students and an adult male. They would learn to use tools, learn the mathematics of measurement and materials, learn the imaginative aspects of design, and learn teamwork.
- reading: as a class, they would get a teacher like me to take them through the novel *Huckleberry Finn*, which would expose them to an outcast like themselves and the cultures along the river.
- survival: a host of mentors would come in to show them how to fish, how to find and eat turtle eggs

like they did in the novel, how to find wild edible foods, and how to protect themselves from the weather.

- entertainment: musicians, jugglers, magicians, dancers, etc. would be involved in having these kids learn acts of various sorts. I will explain why this was part of the plan in the next paragraph.

The rafts without question had to be certified seaworthy and tested because the boys would be spending a good part of the next summer floating down the river on them. They would be accompanied by an adult male figure at the helm, and a motorboat or two would stay with the flotilla for safety reasons. As they floated down the river like Jim and Huck, they would make planned stops at cities along the shore. Here is where the entertainment would come in.

The rafts would be designed with the additional purpose of being stages onshore. Like the King and the Duke of the novel, our students would use the shore for enterprises to make money. But unlike the King and Duke, they wouldn't make money by bilking their audiences, but by singing, dancing, juggling, performing magic, etc. and passing around the hat.

There would be much to learn as these preteens made their trek along the river. Visits to the wild river islands with flora/fauna for study and sources of food. Visits to locks and dams to learn about their workings, and visits to power stations. Further, there would be time to write, draw, and experience nature's spiritual qualities – solitude on the river, the mythology of the night sky, and the ceaseless water flow.

This is a thumbnail sketch of Return to Huckleberry. You say ridiculous, and I have to agree in many ways with you. But as I pointed out in an earlier chapter, I am not only recommending the foolish, I am embracing it. Okay, maybe this project is way out there, but I do believe that education needs to be more way out there and take more risks (I realize all the insurance and legal risks of this project). And I do believe we need to imagine more holistic approaches to engage more students. Once Mark Twain said, "Don't let your schooling get in the way of your education," but I would like to add "Don't let your cowardliness get in the way of your education."

The Thoreauvian

Besides building rafts, my early childhood was filled with building camps, forts, clubhouses, and treehouses – all without any adult supervision. I don't see much of that going on today, but it was quite common for my neighborhood play pals and me to squirrel away whatever materials that were available in the alleyways. Then we'd cut down small trees and large branches for struts in our constructions, using our axes and knives (yes, we all had axes and knives). Then we'd put together dwellings that we looked upon as Camelots when the reality was if parents tried to force us to live in one of these huts, they would have been arrested by Children and Family Services. On one occasion, we almost killed ourselves by attempting to build an underground encampment, when a city official informed us that we were digging into buried power lines. Such was the fever, imagination, and danger that came with our play-work.

When I came upon *Walden Pond* in high school, I was smitten on a new level by Henry David Thoreau's experiment. As an adolescent, it appealed to a desire for self-sufficiency while at the same time a rugged individuality where I could prove my strength by living with nature and in solitude. My fantasies tended toward the American Indian rites of passage, where the teen initiate is sent to the wilderness to live alone and have a vison quest. When he returned, he would be recognized as a man.

Later, in college, I became a votary of R. Buckminster Fuller's geodesic domes, not the huge ones but the smaller versions in *The Whole Earth Catalog*. Eventually, I spent a year building fiberglass, geodesic domes with a surfer in San Clemente, California. We formed a small company and called our domes "The VW of shelter and the Cadillac of tents." The hexagons, pentagons, and half-hexes that made up these domes had a patented locking system, so it could be taken apart and stacked on top of a van to be taken to a new site. Then, it could be re-assembled by two people in 30 minutes. The dome slept 16 people and could be bolted down as a permanent structure.

Building simple and efficient shelters has been a consistent passion of mine, and thus it was quite logical for me to envision holistic classes on shelter building for high school students. Basically, when I thought about such a class, I asked myself WWTD – What Would Thoreau Do? By that, I meant that if H.D. were alive today, how would he go about building a dwelling that could provide all his needs in the simplest and most efficient manner? What materials would he use? There were a lot of new ones out there since Thoreau's time. What design shape – would he build a dome, a yurt, an underground home? What ways would he use to provide himself with energy – wind, solar, water, geothermal, hydrogen? How would he approach food? How would he be economical?

"The Thoreavian," that's my name for the class, would be a class to answer such questions. It would require a great deal of reading, writing, and research of Thoreau and self-sustaining home designs. It would require math and geometry, and the physics of stress and load. The expertise of many teachers and locals would be needed to acquire various kinds of information and building skills. The end goal would be to create, as far as constraints would allow, a self-sustaining dwelling for one person. The class could span a number of years with continuing contributions from future classes until the dwelling could be finished.

The Thoreauvian after that would be used as a one-semester retreat for a selected student to pursue an interest in biology, art, science, writing, etc. The student would live alone in this dwelling with lots of solitude to pursue an interest but also, he or she would have time to attend classes and receive visitors, as Thoreau did himself while living on Walden Pond. The students of the Thoreauvian would keep a journal, and at the end of the semester, they would do a report and presentation about their thoughts, their activities, and their recommendations for improving the house or the experience.

When I began toying with this idea, I was working at a school that had a woods conveniently located nearby. On a number of occasions, I talked casually with the principal and a few board members, asking (supposedly off the cuff), "Wouldn't it be cool to have a class that builds a house like Thoreau's in the forest next door?" Their responses were not tepid; they were zero degrees Kelvin. And what was I to expect? Principals and board members represent the conservative forces in an educational system. Looking to them for imagination is like looking to ostriches for flying lessons.

The creative hut has a long tradition in American intellectual history. Thomas Jefferson had his cabin cottage, John Burroughs his "Slabsides," Buckminster Fuller his rustic home on Bear Island, Wendell Berry his "Long-legged House," and Michael Pollan his "shelter for daydreams." It was my fondest dream that The Thoreavian would join this prestigious parade. But, alas, it was a dream deferred along with Return to Huckleberry. *C'est la vie.*

Conclusion: The Play's the ing

In my defense of my "way-out-there" ideas, I would, first of all, say that they could not be flushed out in the thematic requirements of this book. *Teaching during the Jurassic* is a memoir and not a detailed guide on a curriculum. Secondly, they have never reached the dignified level of failure. There is a quote whose source I have never found, that says, "Christianity has not failed – it has never been tried." I would like to shelter behind a substitution in that quote, "Return to Huckleberry" and "The Thoreauvian" have not failed – they have never been tried.

Further, I don't think that I'm that far off base when I say, "There's a new paradigm for education in the air." In 1998, a classic book for me was Joseph Pine and James Gilmore's *The Experience Economy.* The authors look at the history of economic paradigms in our nation from agriculture to industry to the service industry. It is their contention we are immersed in a new economic paradigm called "the experience economy." In this economy, commodities, goods, and services are not enough; consumers want in addition to all these the creation of memories. A good, fast cup of coffee once sufficed, but no longer; people now want atmosphere, baristas, lattes – and they'll pay more money for them.

If we look at educational systems, we can see that they all succumb to the economic paradigms of their times: the agricultural model giving way to the manufacturing model giving way to the service model. It's no surprise that education has not jumped onto the new experience model, since there is always a lag time between economic innovation and educational acceptance. Sometimes we hold on so dearly to the past that we still have a school calendar based on the agricultural model.

If we continue to hold onto a service model, teachers will be increasingly replaced by long-distance learning, software, and the internet, like industrial workers were replaced by robots. To become part of the experience economy, schools need to "ing the thing." Huh? That means you add *ing* to a product to think about it in terms of giving the user an experience. Thus, coffee becomes coffeeing – a staged experience for the purchase of a cup of coffee; at Starbucks one becomes a kind of tourist rather than a customer. In school, we need to be staging our mathing, booking, historying, etc.

In order to do this, educating needs to as Goethe says, "Be bold and mighty forces will come to your aid." The Thoreauvian and Return to Huckleberry should be looked at as attempts to fail-forward so that schooling can eventually get in line with the world we live in. If I were the education czar today, I would be supporting experiments all over the U.S. to find out what works and what directions in schooling look promising. If this sounds radical, I can only respond I'm a conservative who wants to return to the spirit our country was founded upon, which was radical, democratic, and inventive.

Chapter 14
Ages and Ages Hence

The most misunderstood lines of poetry come from Robert Frost's "The Road Not Taken":

I shall be telling this with a sigh
Somewhere ages and ages hence:
Two roads diverged in a wood, and I –
I took the one less traveled by,
And that has made all the difference.

Many interpret these lines to mean that the narrator's *sigh* is one of contentment because he has chosen the right pathway in life. Thus, we have those who will say, "I took the road less traveled by" as an affirmation of a fulfilled destiny. Yet, the poem is full of indicators ["equally lay," "just as fair," and the problematic, stressed syllables of the last word "difference"] that the narrator is deluding himself into believing his choice was correct, and the sigh is really about wondering what his life would have been if he had taken the other path. It's a poem about doubt and regret.

I have come to the "ages and ages hence" in the poem and, while I have many regrets about the choices I made in my life and while I haven't chosen any kind of unique career path, I sigh over how good I had it, and still have it. Maybe I'm deluding myself, but my time of teaching during the Jurassic has the glow now of mythology and the people that I worked with the stature of demi-gods. In a satisfied dotage, I join the ranks of men who pontificate about the "good ol' days" from a Barcalounger.

I wish I could claim some preternatural ability that guided me into choosing a profession that suited me so well. There are those that have early inklings of what they should be or do in life; I was not one of them. If I had to pick a quote that would characterize my approach to life, it would be Joseph Campbell's, "The fates lead him who will; him who won't they drag." Mostly, I had to be dragged kicking and screaming through the various stages of my life. I am not a wise man but a lucky one.

When everything in your life becomes a feedback loop, you have reached in Maslow's Hierarchy of Needs the stage of Self-actualization. I reached this stage in my teaching career, but certainly not right away. The following chapter is about how many separate threads of my life wove themselves into the teaching life and a whole life.

And Ever the Twain Shall Meet

When you're born on the Mississippi River 15 miles north of Hannibal, Missouri, you will necessarily be baptized in the mythology of Mark Twain. If you're a boy (at least in the 1950s), you will want to build a raft and go down the Mississippi to New Orleans, and you will want to explore the limestone caves in your area (we had them aplenty). By the time you are 12, you will have read *Tom Sawyer* and *Huckleberry Finn* twice and visited all the Twain exhibits in Hannibal several times.

I not only grew up with Mark Twain, but I grew *into* Mark Twain. The more I explored his lesser-known writings, the more I went down the river of humor, wit, and satire with him. Besides Oscar Wilde, I found Samuel Clemens to be the wittiest man that ever lived, and I believed with him, "Humor is mankind's greatest blessing." All that stored up Twain served me well in the teaching profession.

I had a Twain quote on hand to accommodate whatever situation I encountered in school:

- When I was teaching poetry, "The difference between the almost right word and the right word is...the difference between the lightning bug and the lightning."
- If I was teaching research, "There are lies, damned lies and statistics."
- When I was teaching speech, "It usually takes me more than three weeks to prepare a good impromptu speech."
- When I had my students read the Classics, "'Classic.' A book which people praise and don't read."
- When I was trying to give students a larger perspective on the world, "I never let my schooling interfere with my education."

- If I was disciplining students, "It is better to keep your mouth closed and let people think you are a fool than to open it and remove all doubt."
- If I was in the faculty lounge, "In the first place, God made idiots. That was for practice. Then he made school boards."
- When I was talking to the administration about the progress of a particular class, "Everything has its limit – iron ore cannot be educated into gold."

In addition to Mark Twain, I was raised in another tradition of humor that came from the family business. My father ran quite a few different taverns as I was growing up until we settled in (one of the names of his bars was the "Settle Inn") to a restaurant and bar business that lasted for decades. Before I could see above a bar top, I was behind the bar, helping my dad in one way or another.

The culture of the liquor is conducive to becoming entertaining. Stories that try to capture an audience are being told all the time at the bar, and the majority of them are humorous. I took in these anecdotes and jokes like a sponge. My popularity in grade school and high school (we had no middle school) had a lot to do with my knowing so many funny stories. Then there was the doggerel. My father was a fount of toasts and off-color poems.

Of course, I witnessed the kind of appreciation he received when he recited these, and he recited them so often that it was easy for me to memorize them. His elocution of these poems was flawless, and the gestures and postures that accompanied them were of high oration. It was all part of the mock seriousness of the themes. As you would expect, I passed these along to my buddies in school, who found them outrageously funny but were unable to copy them as they could my jokes. If someone wanted to hear the work of the bards of the bar, they had to come to me.

While you would think that most of this low form of humor wouldn't have a lot of application to my life as a teacher, it was profound. First of all, I wouldn't have gone into English, if I didn't have an appreciation for a good story and the *artfulness* of telling a good story. I realized early on that two people could tell the same joke, and one would get laughs and the other would fall flat. It all had to do with the art of delivery, which I learned at the foot of the masters at the bar. My sense of what a good story was and of what good technique was evolved into an appreciation of the greatest storytellers of all – the literary giants.

Secondly, I had memorized some lengthy doggerel and the delivery techniques that went with them. As I became engaged in more challenging kinds of verse, I knew how to memorize and how to recite. Both of these skills became a staple in all my classes whether Robert Frost poems or Shakespearean soliloquies. Also, I was ready with a poem for times in the students' lives that required eloquence. I love reciting an excerpt from Walt Whitman's "Song of the Open Road" to seniors going out into the world:

...light-hearted I take to the open road,
Healthy, free, the world before me,
The long brown path before me leading wherever I choose.
Henceforth I ask not good-fortune, I myself am good-fortune,
Henceforth I whimper no more, postpone no more, need
    nothing,

Done with indoor complaints, libraries, querulous criticisms,
Strong and content I travel the open road.

These two sources, Mark Twain and the bar trade, translated well to the classroom. While it would not be a requirement to be entertaining in the classroom, I was entertaining. I loved captivating students with good stories, memorized poems, and humor. It was a legacy I received from a river and a restaurant in Illinois. A legacy that I have spent and keep on spending.

Yearning and Learning

There is a developmental period in adolescence that manifests itself as a pervasive longing. It's intertwined with the desires of sexual development and the desire to prove oneself by doing something heroic. This yearning for me as a high school student was like the green light in *The Great Gatsby* – it represented both an ideal girl and my highest aspirations.

I changed a great deal during my high school years. In grade school (K-8), I was smart enough, but I didn't devote much time to my studies. But in high school, I became an insatiable learner. Behind this change was the idea that I would become beloved by society and *the girl* because of the deepness of my understanding. Society and *the girl* could count on my superior intellect to guide them. Corny as it sounds (aren't all these gestures of teens toward the ideal), it was the beginning of my journey to becoming a teacher.

My devotion to learning was not like a rifle, narrow and precise. It was more like the spray of a shotgun. I was interested in everything – physics as well as literature, algebra as well as history, tap dancing as well as basketball. It was all one fabric to me. As I became acquainted with so many areas of learning both in and out of school, I had absolutely no notion of this leading to a career or a means of making money. It had everything to do with passion.

As I continued on into college, I remained a generalist of knowledge. ("Please, don't ask me to pick a major.") At the end of my first four years of college, I graduated with 150 hours, 30 more than required. Since I was forced to pick a major, I chose English in my last year and backed it up with a teaching certificate as demanded by my advisor.

My all-consuming desire to know was not suppressed by the uniformity and conformity of the military. I was still able to follow my bliss, as Joseph Campbell would recommend. I remember that after a day of physical activity in Basic Training, I still had energy enough to run to the fort's library and read, enfolded in its mahogany tables and pools of light. While training in the hospital at Ft. Bliss (nothing to do with Joseph Campbell's bliss), I learned the basics of the Vietnamese language. In the hospital, I passed tests in physical therapy and occupational therapy.

As soon as I was out of the service, I was on the road like Kerouac and Cassady. I lived in my van while I took a photography course in Aspen's Center for the Eye. In San Clemente, California, I built geodesic domes out of fiberglass. Who knows how long I could have continued this pinball machine existence? I was a votary of e. e. cummings, "follow no paths/ all paths lead to where. truth is here." But then I received a phone call from the career center at my college. Mr. Chaney, a guy I had always liked and who was a regular at our restaurant, told me there was an English teacher opening in a high school near to my hometown and asked if I would be interested. They needed someone right away because the teacher that they originally hired had quit because of an illness. Since I was strapped for cash and getting tired of living in my van, I thought why not try it out for a year. I interviewed and got the job. And that became the inauspicious beginning of a lifelong career.

When I began to teach, I realized this large ball of string made from the many pieces of my "schooling and education" (Twain) would now have application. Again, with no

insight or foresight into my future, I was lucky that I had an English degree and a teaching certificate. English had the necessary scope for me to bring in knowledge and experiences from a variety of sources; science and math did not offer such flexibility. For example:

- Building portable geodesic domes in San Clemente was a great entrée into *Walden Pond* and the economical domicile that Thoreau built.
- Visiting communes in my travels like Thane Walker's The Prosperos and working at a Trappist Monastery in Conyers, Georgia, became class material for the utopias in *Brave New World* and *Walden Two*.
- Magic tricks that I learned at the bar and from reading magic books came in handy as reading material for remedial English. I would interest students in a magic trick, but the only way that they could discover how it was done was by

reading a description of it. Then, they had to perform it for me. Comprehension assured.

- The tap-dancing that I could do helped with the choreography of the musicals that I directed.

- My knowledge of visual perception helped me bring together literature, art, and music. William Faulkner's four narrators in *The Sound and the Fury* was a modern perceptual device that paralleled the Cubists. The etiology of the name for the rock group *The Doors* went through Aldous Huxley's *Doors of Perception*, which in turn came from the 18th-century artist/poet William Blake's poem "The Marriage of Heaven and Hell."

- Experiences in the army hospitals allowed me to talk about the phantom limb syndrome in conjunction with Whitman and Melville: Whitman witnessing this syndrome as a Civil War nurse; Melville having Ahab complain of still feeling the leg that Moby Dick bit off.

- When I became a yearbook sponsor, the photography courses that I had taken resulted in my putting in a photo lab so that we could develop our own pictures instead of sending them out. That, in turn, became the basis for general classes in photography for the student body.

I couldn't make an exhaustive list if I wanted to, but the list above illustrates how there is no useless knowledge. All knowledge fuses rather well together and facts are tools in a shed that can be used for all sorts of purposes. I never found in education a separation between the sciences and the humanities; I never found a separation between the depths that could be attained in any line of work and the work of educators. I often told people that I had a bar degree because of the many years I had spent as a bartender. I was only half kidding because my time spent behind the bar taught me as much as any of my college degrees.

As a generalist learner, I had found a niche of expression in the teaching profession. I wanted to be an English teacher in the same kind of inclusive and energetic way as the books *The Medium Is the Massage* and *I Seem To Be a Verb* (collaborations of Quentin Fiore with Marshall McLuhan and Buckminster Fuller, respectively). Only in retrospect could I finally say, "I was born to teach."

Getting Ten-year

There's a dictum in teaching, which says, "It takes three years before you can teach a new course." The first year you are engaged on a daily basis on the mechanics of lesson plans, materials, and what works or doesn't work. In the second year, you have your first year's lesson plans and experiences, but you realize that you're still quite far away from having control of the material so that you can deliver it in a "spontaneous" way. The third year, you're in control and armed with all the knowledge of two years of pitfalls, trials, and practice.

When you're a brand-new teacher, you have to go through the three-year cycle with *all* your courses, not just one new one. The incline of the learning curve is quite sharp, and many new teachers are sowed among the thorns and choked out before they really get a good start. But if you come out on the other side of these three years, your life becomes more of an even stride than a series of mad dashes. This happened to me as I was integrated into the rhythm of work of a high school English teacher. Looking back, I was surprised the school system decided to rehire me during my first couple of years, since I made so many mistakes. But by my third year, I walked tall as a professional.

I would like to add another dictum to the three-year dictum, the ten-year dictum. After ten years as an instructor, I had become like an improvisational jazz musician. Writing my lesson plans became a creative exercise like writing musical scores. Further, they might be musical compositions that I never used. I had the ability to go off on a tangent if I thought the direction of the class was improved thereby. I felt no strict obligation to stick to what I had prepared or to "cover the material." If a student asked a *real* question (this only happened a couple of times during a semester), I would veer from my plans to give him or her an answer or try to pose the question to the class for discussion. If there were events in society of some importance – fights for equality by marginalized groups, the Roe v. Wade Supreme Court decision, the Jonestown Massacre, *Star Wars*, Vietnam War Memorial, Chernobyl, etc., I would go off script and allow class time for engagement of these contemporary issues.

My home life, my hobbies, my work time, and my time in the car all became a homeostasis – feedback systems mutually reinforcing each other. Whatever I read for myself became material for my classes; whatever I read for my classes became reading material for my life. My vacations were influenced by what I taught. In the summer, I made a pilgrimage to Thoreau's cabin and Walden Pond, baptizing myself in its holy, literary waters.

The pictures of my vacation were hung in both my home and at school – here's Mr. Settle and his family at Edgar Allan Poe's dorm room at the University of Virginia.

The clothes I wore became a method of teaching. At one point in my career, I had over 20 T-shirts custom-made that I would wear over my dress shirts. They would have quotes written on the front or back that begged engagement from students (and even teachers and administrators). For instance, "Eppur si muove" printed on the back of one T-shirt. No one could resist asking what that meant. It meant "And yet it moves"; it was attributed to Galileo after he recanted to Pope Urban VIII his claims about a heliocentric solar system (the quote was supposedly said under his breath). Many kinds of discussions and writing assignments could be introduced using this T-shirt: John Greenleaf Whittier threw Walt Whitman's *Leaves of Grass* into his fireplace as trash; during Emily Dickinson's life, she hardly published a poem and was told not to publish her work by Thomas Wentworth Higginson, the editor of *The Atlantic*; that no one believed the hobbyist scientist Antony van Leeuwenhoek that there was a multitude of creatures in a drop of water; that the French Impressionists were forced to show their work in the Salon of the Refused. Writing prompt – "What is another example in history when the people of the time assumed one thing was true, but it was not true, and what might be an example of this in our own times." Further, not only did I wear T-shirts to school, but out in public. They always yielded many interesting encounters with strangers.

If I went shopping, I would use the grammar and spelling mistakes of advertising as examples for my classes. I was always prepared for inspiration and epiphany, carrying a small, top-bound notebook and golf pencil like Jack Kerouac so that I could write them down immediately. I told my friends that if I died on the highway, it would probably be the result of writing an idea in a notebook while I was driving. It's amazing how many problems are solved, or good ideas pop up while you're driving. It is equally amazing how many of those inspirations are lost by the time you reach your destination if you haven't written them down.

For me, becoming a ten-yeared teacher meant that my personal, social, and academic lives had become melded in such a way that it was difficult to tell where one left off and the other began. I was moving toward self-actualization.

Conclusion: Dream on

How beautifully my career as an English teacher, both in high school and college, has seamlessly flowed into retirement. I have watched others outside the profession heading into that pasture with all kinds of trepidations and identity crises. Not so for me.

First, I realized that in many ways, I was becoming a dinosaur of the Jurassic. I did not have the intuitive skills necessary for the new technologies nor did I understand the zeitgeist of the new generation. After I hit my 60s, I began getting plain tired of keeping up with software and finding ways to use it creatively. So, as much as we all like to fight time, I had to accept that I was getting old and my growth rings were splitting my bark.

Secondly, I decided it was okay now to be selfish. I had done my stint for society in helping birth students into good thinkers and good citizens. I had many areas that I would

like to explore without having to take notes to see how I was going to use what I had learned in the classroom. And there was so much to explore!

The grazing grounds of knowledge go off into infinity, and learning is what brought me to teaching in the first place. I would have no trouble retiring because I had so much to graze upon in those pastures. As so many dedicated readers will tell you, they almost despair going into a Barnes and Noble, seeing all the books that they would love to read and realizing that they'd have to live to be a thousand to get the job done. On the other side of this dilemma, however, is the reassuring thought that you will never be bored, which is the case for me.

Besides reading in my retirement, one must remember that I was an English teacher to my fingertips. All English teachers to their fingertips have a secret desire to become like the writers they have taught and to write something beautiful or profound themselves. I wanted to be like Norman Maclean, a retired English teacher, who wrote his first novel at 74, *A River Runs Through It*. Not bad for a first try. Thus, in my twilight years, I have taken itchy fingertips to the keyboard, as this book demonstrates. Of this writing, I have published four books of poetry and self-published one multimedia book on the alphabet. I have many future books stored in the hopper and will probably continue to write as I drool on a draft in a nursing home.

One of the great surprises in my retirement is that I have a knack for assemblage art (that's art that makes sculptures out of junk). In the beginning, I worked on these sculptures in the house, but as my projects grew in quantity and size and my wife was tired of tripping over them in the house, we built a studio in the backyard. My wife likes it when I am out there tinkering. She has offered to put in plumbing, a kitchen, and a bed. ("Nice try, Dear, but you're not going to get rid of me that easily.")

While I sigh for all the lives I could have lived, I sigh, also, because of what a good life teaching has provided me. I still reflect on all the lessons that I learned so intimately in the profession, and I still keep in contact with former colleagues and students, who are now much older than I was when I taught them. And while I do not go into the future like Tennyson's Ulysses, an old man that thinks he still can be what he was, I do not go without a desire to continue achieving and accomplishing. I wish I could be a man comfortable with the Eastern practices of meditation and living in the now. All my life I have tried various methods to be attuned to some inner, mystical side, but I have always failed miserably. There is nothing like a mantra and deep breathing to induce sleep for me and, while I like to stretch, they haven't invented the yoga class that I was suited for, which would be named something like "Hurry-up Yoga."

No, I am a Westerner through and through – goal-oriented and besotted with rational thought. I am filled with utopias and ameliorations for the world. It has always been a puzzle to me why society is not consumed with beauty and learning, and that we have such violence emerging everywhere. My life as an English instructor has been a commitment to inspire the new life with dreams that will sustain them and ultimately the planet. So many teachers in my past have given me such gifts.

As I have said in an earlier chapter, "Notes from Pisgah," I am disappointed that we have not gone farther along the road of educational change. With all our new technologies, information flow, and political freedom, we lack not only imagination but the will to try the imaginative. Using a Marshall McLuhan analogy, we are driving into the future looking at our rearview mirrors. Unlike our country's founders and pioneers, we refuse to live in a different way.

Education is the unending journey – always exciting and always a bit fearful. I hope that we find today's crossroads in education full of opportunity. As Wendell Berry has said, "It may be that when we no longer know which way to go that we have come to our real journey. The mind that is not baffled is not employed. The impeded stream is the one that sings." Let us sing as we go about re-visioning education. I feel a song coming on.

Epilogue
Principals from the Principle

If you have read the "Prankenstein" chapter in this book, you will understand my choice of this title for the epilogue. The epilogue will be my parting epigrams about teaching and education. You will find some quotes right out of the chapters; some influenced by the themes of the chapters; and some that take on new territory. Unlike "Principals from the Principal," I try to be insightful and sometimes inciteful. Gather as ye may – the pith of a good quote is an alligator in the moat. You may quote me on that.

Median, Mean, and the Commode

Efficiency and accountability are the last refuge of schools without vision.

Efficiency and accountability make teachers into bureaucrats.

You can measure training results; you cannot measure teaching results.

Training is mechanical; learning is erotic.

Training is not the same as teaching. Teaching tries to impart knowledge at the gut level.

The common experience of many great thinkers, artists, and scientists is not so much their individual genius or the prestige of a school that they attended but having a great teacher.

New teachers should not be thrown to the wolves but coddled in an apprenticeship.

The best teachers need to be rotated occasionally into the very worst schools. They also need to run these schools.

There is no substitute for face-to-face evaluation of a student's understanding. Each student should pass an oral exam in front of a committee of teachers before he or she can graduate.

All children are left behind if the school is concerned with numbers. Let us document how much a waste of time documenting is, and then flush those documents down the commode.

Leave No Politician Behind

Can there be any doubt that politicians do not understand teachers and don't understand education?
As educators, we need to adopt this political stance: no politician left behind.

Putting money and resources into education is much more important to our society's future than putting money and resources into its military defense.

The capitalistic motive is reductive at best. Public schools should have nothing to do with privatization or voucher systems.

Merit pay is always meretricious.

No more mega-schools. A good size for a school is around 500.

Those that can, teach; those that could, need more money.

Throwing money at a problem...is not a bad idea.

All politicians who think teachers should not be paid more should have to switch jobs with a teacher for one semester.

Education Myths

Myth: If it is humorous, it can't be educational.

Myth: There is no difference in the learning experience between 20 and 40 students in the classroom.

Myth: Lots of homework is a measure of quality education.

Myth: All the important aspects of learning can be measured.

Myth: Computers improve writing and learning directly.

Myth: Charter schools are superior to Public Schools.

Myth: A teaching degree is all that is required to be a good teacher.

Myth: With our new technologies, our schools are cutting edge.

Artful Dodgers

The arts are not ancillary to education; they are the heart of education.

Put more money into the arts than into your sports programs.

Literature is as short as it can be; there is no summary of it.

Not only is a movie not a substitute for the book, but it is often a misrepresentation of the book.

Entire works of literature should be read rather than bits and pieces from anthologies. Better to go the way of depth than trivia.

The privilege of the English teacher is that at the heart of all education is the story, and humans are wired for stories.

Music should have an important place across the curriculum.

The architecture of the school is a blueprint of the philosophy of the school.

Trailer classrooms are symbols of the low status of education. Think about visiting a lawyer or doctor located in a trailer.

Hidden Wells of Incompetency

The fewer the administrators, the better.

Administrators should come from the ranks of academic educators, not from coaches or ex-military officers.

Pay teachers more to get good teachers. Pay administrators the same as teachers to get good administrators.

What we can do about education is give it back to the teachers.

If you want to retain teachers, you must give them the autonomy that implies they are professionals and competent.

The Public School System is as much of an inspired creation as our three branches of government, and our democracy depends just as much on it.

Administrators are a creatively challenged group.

I have always found that administrators get in the way of most education. My philosophy was just leave me alone, and I will get a lot more done.

"Hurting our numbers" is an accountancy phrase. Administrators use it to ask teachers to do unethical things like inflating grades.

Excellence cannot be hidden long; incompetency can be hidden for a lot longer.

Designing Discipline

Nurture the trickster. Mischief helps the medicine go down.

School spirit cannot be demanded of students. School spirit exists only if a school has spirit.

There is no better discipline than keeping students after school to get to know them.

Adulthood should come earlier for adolescents.

Disciplinary actions should be swift and sure.

A discipline too loose loses content; a discipline too tight loses imagination.

All education should combine wonder and discipline. Wonder should come before discipline because it leads to the willingness to be disciplined.

Order and uniformity are virtues in the military, not in education. Education is messy. Fascism likes to do things one way.

Imagination Unbound

Imagination is the highest and most difficult thing we teach.

First, you must see the box before you can think outside it.

Categories can be unmade because they are manmade.

Pulling on a thread of knowledge can lead to untangling a knot or dismantling a category.

It takes imagination to teach about imagination.

Being prepared for inspiration means carrying a notebook.

The "Ah-ha" or Eureka experience in the classroom is a teacher's cocaine.

Daydreaming is a necessary part of the school day.

Imagination is what will save our nation in the future.

The discrete increments of learning eventually become synergistic explosions.

Caveat Magister

Beware the good-old-daze.

Beware the loner.

Beware college professors that have not taught high school yet write books for it.

Beware of going through the motions as a teacher. Going through the motions is losing the emotions upon which real learning depends.

Beware of equating memorizing facts with teaching.

Beware of any privatization of public education.

Admonitions and Additions

Eliminate clocks and bells.

Eliminate grades.

Recitation should be a part of every curriculum.

All students should be required to take chorus or a least some collective enterprise that is not a team sport.

Students should drop off all cell phones before entering the school.

Have one or more parents of students in class all the time.

All students should leave school with competency.

It is important to have places for silence in a school.

Let humorous help onerous.

Inconvenient Truths

Critical thinking should include criticism of our nation's history.

The imperfections of great people should be pointed out to students so that they can realistically measure their contributions.

History should be unflinchingly truthful and include those chapters of our nation's past that we are ashamed of.

The educational system is being held back by a false sense of patriotism and of religion.

Public schools should remain quiet about God and shout out Reason. God and Reason are not exclusive of one another, but they should be learned in different buildings.

Separation of church and state means they have their separate spheres in a person's education.

Time to move on: Evolution in public education should never be skirted but embraced as one of the all-time great ideas in science. If you think this is debatable, start your own school.

Climate change is indisputable unless you think that science is an irrelevant part of the curriculum.

Mental Perturbations

There should be proportionally more psychologists and special ed teachers in low-income schools than other schools.

You can substitute teachers; you cannot substitute a good home life.

Dear parents, criticizing your children causes more damage to your children than broken bones.

Children sitting all day are like animals in captivity.

It is difficult after lunch to determine whether the sleepiness in a class is the result of digestion or your teaching. Gastronomy recapitulates pedagogy.

If you want to grow, you need to make an ass of yourself on a regular basis.

Hell is the first place you go to before you are enlightened.

Daily drama, thy name is teenager.

Some days you look at the clock to see if the second hand is moving.

Screwing up makes for good stories.

Just for Sport

Why is it that they always threaten to get rid of band and the arts to encourage people to vote for a school bond? If you want to threaten to get rid of programs, threaten to eliminate the sports programs. Then, see the support come pouring in.

Sports programs are not as important as introducing the practices of exercise and recreational sports into all students' lives.

Hire coaches that are teachers first and coaches second.

Restrict coaches from the driver's training, P.E., and history triad as their teaching load.

Monies for sports should not be lopsided in favor of one sport.

Coaching salaries should not be lopsided in favor of one sport.

More important than winning are the values of cooperation and comradery of team sports.

An important aspect of sports is that it can be a rite of passage for many teens.

Simplicity Given and Earned

You can tell how well you know something when you teach it. If you cannot simplify it, you don't know it.

You must go through a lot of complexity to arrive at a simple solution.

The simple essence of school is questions: answering questions, creating questions, developing ways to answer questions, and questioning your answers.

The teaching experience is transformative: the simplicity you seek to teach your students is the same simplicity that you must find in yourself.

Why do we struggle so mightily to teach foreign languages when the simple solution would be to immerse a very young child in a playgroup with children speaking another language?

Whatever the technology, there is only understanding or not understanding.

Portals to Thought

Multiculturalism is an imperative goal for all schools.

Multiculturalism is relevant to all content areas.

Multiculturalism is the key to entering all postmodern philosophies: Deconstructionism, Structuralism, Social Constructivism, etc.

Teachers create the vacuums that educe students; that is, students sometimes have to be sucked into learning.

Only the seized person can seize others.

There is no substitute for raw interest.

Try to define the challenges of your times. Then bring them into your classroom.

Different educational approaches and different teacher personalities are required to open up different minds.

Assessment Rules

Covering material is often smothering material.

Poor teachers can mold minds.

Students should write in their books. Marginalia is not marginal; it is the reader's engagement with the material.

If you teach grammar with a hammer, you're screwed. Grammar is not an isolated field; it must be taught with semantics.

New technologies have not improved student writing a whit, a jot, or a tittle.

Hour for hour there's better money in being a barista than a yearbook sponsor.

Faculty lounges are a necessity, not a luxury.

All levels of teaching should have semester sabbaticals.

Arming teachers is like having the police carry thesauruses.

From Data to Goodness

Data is individual facts; information is the categorizing of data; knowledge is the power that comes from understanding information; wisdom is the proper use of power that comes from knowledge. None should be left out of education.

Data can be a good way of lying.

Information that does not in-form is data.

There is no useless knowledge.

Outdated does not mean useless.

All wisdom is ecology.

About Atmosphere Press

Atmosphere Press is an independent, full-service publisher for excellent books in all genres and for all audiences. Learn more about what we do at atmospherepress.com.

We encourage you to check out some of Atmosphere's latest releases, which are available at Amazon.com and via order from your local bookstore:

About the Author

Martin Settle is a retired English teacher. In the past 32 years, he has taught elementary school, middle school, high school, and college. Settle has published five books: *The Teleology of Dunes*, *Coming to Attention: Developing the Habit of Haiku*, *The Backbone Alphabet*, *Maple Samaras* and *The Metaphorest*. Martin has received The Thomas McDill Award for Poetry, the Nazim Hikmet Poetry Award, the Griffin-Farlow Haiku Award, and the North Carolina Poetry Society's Poetry of Courage Award. In addition to his books, he has published a multitude of poems and educational articles.

Learn more at www.martinsettleartist.com

CPSIA information can be obtained
at www.ICGtesting.com
Printed in the USA
FSHW011803030821
83591FS